D0975516

THERAPEUTIC METAPHORS

THERAPEUTIC METAPHORS

*Helping Others
Through The
Looking Glass*

by David Gordon

META Publications
Cupertino, California 95014

International Standard Book Number: 0-916990-04-4
Library of Congress Catalog Card Number: 78-58574
META Publications, Cupertino, California 95014

Designed by Hester Greene
Typography by Editorial Associates, Los Altos, Calif.
Frontispiece illustration by Dana Roberts

To
Richard Bandler and John Grinder,
Both of whom I love, like, and
Respect very much...

...and that's not just a way of talking about them

CONTENTS

FOREWORD

As long as recorded history has been around, and in myths that date back into the farthest and dimmest memories of human existence, metaphor has been used as a mechanism of teaching and of changing ideas. Shamen, philosophers, and prophets alike have intuitively known and used the power of the metaphor. From Plato's allegory of the cave right through to Voltaire's Zagdig, from the teachings of Jesus and Buddha to the teachings of Don Juan, metaphor is ever present as a tool for changing ideas and affecting behavior. It then comes as no surprise to me to find the use of metaphor in the behavior of the intuitive clinician, the "modern" practitioner of psychotherapy. This book by David Gordon represents one of the first steps forward in making the intuitive use of metaphor explicit and, therefore, available as a tool to a greater number of professional communicators. It is my belief that this endeavor represents the opportunity for all of us who are interested in expanding both our understanding and effectiveness as communicators the chance to become more adept and creative with our use of metaphor as a tool of teaching and behavioral change.

I remember early in my career as a modeler of psychotherapy being quite amazed at the number of "professionals" who would come to me to learn the patterns of communication we had extracted from exquisite communicators in the field . . . professionals who would spend their time debating the effectiveness and usefulness of techniques they themselves had not yet tried. In the beginning I debated back and found it pointless, so I began demanding that these professionals try the patterns themselves before discussion. This of course led to further discussion. Finally deciding that the futility of my efforts was based upon my own

behavior, I began telling stories about a professor I had had in
college, Melvin Stewart, biologist *par excellence.* Melvin's main
interest in biology during my college days was the study of desert
terrain. He would take small groups of young, flourishing biolo-
gists down into the desert for intensive study. Most of the time
these trips were uneventful, although they did serve an educational
need. However one summer, miles from civilization, the land rover
broke down. It was therefore necessary for Melvin and his young
crew to set out on foot to find their way back to get help. They
took with them only the essentials for survival—food, water, and
maps. According to the maps they would have to hike for about
three days to reach the nearest signpost of civilization. So the trek
began. Marching, resting, then marching again this solemn and
determined group proceeded through the hot wilderness. On the
morning of the third day a tired and worn out group reached the
summit of a huge sand dune. Thirsty and sunburned, they began
to view the terrain about them. Far off to their right was what
appeared to be a lake with small trees surrounding it. The students
jumped and screamed for joy, but Melvin did not. He knew that
it was only a mirage. He had been here before, he said to himself.
He presented the bad news (as would any professor) as facts that
had to be accepted. His students, however, rebelled and insisted
they knew what they were seeing. The argument continued until
Melvin was worn to a frazzle. Finally he conceded to let the students go out to the mirage, after obtaining a promise from them
that once they discovered it was a mirage they would sit down
and not move until he returned with help. Each student swore that
they would wait and not wander any further. Melvin went his
way . . . and the students went theirs. Three hours later the students arrived at a plush new desert resort which had four swim-
ming pools and six restaurants. Two hours after that they set out
in a land rover with the rangers in search of Melvin, who was never
found. I received an incomplete in biology. I never again was
forced to argue the merits of trying over talking in a training
seminar. As you the reader of this volume are faced with the
delightful opportunity to read a book both well thought out and

well written you are also at a crossroad. You may read this book as you would any other, or you can realize that this is just one more unprecedented opportunity to expand the range and skill you now have as a communicator both to affect ideas and change behavior. As when you reach any crossroad, any point of moving in new directions, there is a possibility that the promises of destination are only mirages floating on the wings of time . . . however, can any of you really afford to take that chance? The practical knowledge available in this volume is disguised as enjoyable reading that may be seen, heard, and felt, but, even more importantly, may it be used.

> *As sincerely as possible,*
> *Richard Bandler*

PART I
INTRODUCTION

PROLOGUE

from

Alice in Wonderland

by Lewis Carroll

There was a table set out under a tree in front of the house, and the March Hare and the Hatter were having tea at it: a Dormouse was sitting between them, fast asleep, and the other two were using it as a cushion, resting their elbows on it, and talking over its head. "Very uncomfortable for the Dormouse," thought Alice; "only, as it's asleep, I suppose it doesn't mind."

The table was a large one, but the three were all crowded together at one corner of it. "No room! No room!" they cried out when they saw Alice coming. "There's *plenty* of room!" said Alice indignantly, and she sat down in a large arm-chair at one end of the table.

"Have some wine," the March Hare said in an encouraging tone.

Alice looked all round the table, but there was nothing on it but tea. "I don't see any wine," she remarked.

"There isn't any," said the March Hare.

"Then it wasn't very civil of you to offer it," said Alice angrily.

"It wasn't very civil of you to sit down without being invited," said the March Hare.

"I didn't know it was *your* table," said Alice: "it's laid for a great many more than three."

"Your hair wants cutting," said the Hatter. He had been looking at Alice for some time with great curiosity, and this was his first speech.

"You should learn not to make personal remarks," Alice said with some severity: "It's very rude.

The Hatter opened his eyes very wide on hearing this; but all he *said* was, "Why is a raven like a writing-desk?"

"Come, we shall have some fun now!" thought Alice. "I'm glad they've begun asking riddles—I believe I can guess that," she added aloud.

"Do you mean that you think you can find out the answer to it?" said the March Hare.

"Exactly so," said Alice.

"Then you should say what you mean," the March Hare went on.

"I do," Alice Hastily replied; "at least—at least I mean what I say—that's the same thing, you know."

"Not the same thing a bit!" said the Hatter. "Why, you might just as well say that 'I see what I eat' is the same thing as 'I eat what I see'!"

"You might just as well say," added the March Hare, "that 'I like what I get' is the same thing as 'I get what I like'!"

"You might just as well say," added the Dormouse, which seemed to be talking in its sleep, "that 'I breathe when I sleep' is the same thing as 'I sleep when I breathe'!"

"It *is* the same thing with you," said the Hatter, and here the conversation dropped, and the party sat silent for a minute, while Alice thought over all she could remember about ravens and writing desks, which wasn't much.

INTRODUCTION

Long, long ago, in a special time and in a particular place a man sat before an intent assemblage of his contemporaries and told stories to them. The story-teller's audience could have been paupers or princes. That did not matter, for the tales the man wove were tailored for all whose cloth of life may have torn, tattered, or worn thin. Some had been exposed to the cold here, others to a malevolent eye there, and still others had wardrobes that were drab or unsuitable.

What the story-teller wove on his loom of dramatic gestures, meaningful pauses (glancing from face to face, of course), and impromptu histrionics, was a tapestry that contained characters suitably good and evil who rushed wide-eyed and headlong (or blindly stumbled) into . . . into what? Why, an adventure of course. Perhaps it was a voyage, or a meeting with a rock. Perhaps there was a luscious maiden, or a boorish barfly. Or even a god. Or even God. But always, always an adventure. Some previously uncharted territory between two oceans or between two ears is trekked. The reward for these sojourns is the excitement of taking chances and the perspective gained from having taken those chances.

And so our story-teller tells us of a long-besieged walled city. Both within and without those walls men show bravery and cowardice, brotherhood and treachery, piety and blasphemy. They try to kill one another—sometimes out of vengeance, and sometimes out of pity. At times they speak with more wisdom and forebearance than they themselves can account for. At other times they are foolish and petty. And always they are doing the best they can with the sensibilities and sensitivities they each have. And one of these men leads a ship home after the warring has ended. The story-teller describes for us the awesome array of temptations and pitfalls which interpose themselves between this war-weary sailor and his home. Our sailor overcomes each danger in turn, of course, and with each victory his resourcefulness, courage, and integrity grow. Now, you object that these adventures are no doubt very exciting and "therapeutic" for our struggling wayfarer, but of what use are his exploits to me? Ahhh! The story-teller looks down, strokes his chin whiskers, and smiles. Ahhh, he repeats, and, as he scratches his throat, he explains to you that in the course of his own wanderings he has discovered that when he tells his tales, those who listen actually *live those adventures* inside of themselves. In fact, he continues (and here he looks up at you with mischievous eyes), in fact people are living amazing adventures all the time.

Stories in one form or another have been used by human beings for countless ages as a means of transmitting important cultural, sociological, and moral information from one generation to the next. Homer's tales were laced with important lessons for his contemporaries on the "proper" ways to think and behave. He taught (or reminded) them how to properly treat a stranger or a relative, face danger and hardship, worship, and so on. Similarly, the fables of Aesop and Da Vinci ranged in subject matter from comments upon the quirks of human nature to considering the meaning of existence.

Although the content of these tales may vary, there is no essential structural difference between the *Odyssey*, *Alice in Wonderland*, and Carlos Casteneda's experiences with Don Juan. All describe individuals, real or imagined, who are confronted with problems which demand that Odysseus, Alice, and Carlos each tap their personal resources in order to overcome those problems. The parallels between their adventures and the myriad of problems which we as fellow human beings are confronted with is usually obvious. The solutions Odysseus develops for himself may not be acceptable to some individuals, but that he is grappling with situations with which most of us are acquainted cannot be denied.

Have you ever felt yourself between the rocks of Scylla and Charybdis regarding a particular decision? Or attracted to a siren whom you somehow knew would lead you to destruction? Or perhaps some particular experience out of your past is an Achilles heel for you? Such parallels between fable and human experience are often so consistent and widespread that they are assimilated into languages as idioms. In one form or another each of us deals daily with Pandora's box, Serpents proffering apples, Sleeping Beauties and Prince Charmings.

Such stories, anecdotes, and idioms all have as a constituent part the ability to convey a message or learning about a particular problem. *Someone* is confronted with *some problem* which he/she/it overcomes (or succumbs to) in *some way.* The way in which the protagonist resolves the problem can provide a possible solution for others in a similar bind. If the conflict within the story is similar to one you as a listener happen also to be dealing with, then the story immediately becomes more significant for you. You may have had the experience, while listening to an anecdote or tale, of identifying various characters within the story with people or things that are actually familiar to you. It is likely that with such associations you also felt particularly curious about the story's resolution. Examples of the sources of such "stories" include epic poems, novels, poetry, fairy tales, fables, parables, songs, movies, jokes, and gossip.

When any of these story-sources are presented with the intention of instructing or advising the listener, or if the listener implies for himself such an advisory relationship, then that story becomes for that person a METAPHOR. In his book, *Guru: Metaphors from a Psychotherapist*, Sheldon Kopp defines "metaphor" as follows:

> Generally, a metaphor is defined as a way of speaking in which one thing is expressed in terms of another, whereby this bringing together throws new light on the character of what is being described. (p. 17)

A metaphor, then, is a *novel representation* of something (the old saying that "there is more than one way to skin a cat" comes to mind). Kopp goes on to explore the metaphorical implications of such story-sources as mythology, religion, literature, science fiction, the media, and pop culture. His conception of metaphor as a wide-ranging source of "new light" on old concerns is one which we can profitably use here in the context of therapeutic metaphors. Similar themes have been explored by such philosopher-psychologists as Erich Fromm in his *The Forgotten Language*, Joseph Campbell in his *The Hero with a Thousand Faces*, Bettelheim's *The Uses of Enchantment*, and in the many volumes which have been written on dream interpretation. As useful as all of these treatises are in helping us understand the literary, aesthetic, and therapeutic significance of "standard" and traditional metaphors, until now no volume has as yet been produced which describes how to *formulate* complex metaphors. The purpose of this book is to provide you with skills which will enable you to formulate and effectively use therapeutic metaphors.

SECTION 1
The Metaphor "Metaphor"

All therapeutic approaches and systems make explicit and implicit use of metaphors. An example is Freud's use of sexual symbolism as a means of decoding dreams, fantasies, and "unconscious" associations. Jung developed the "animus" and the "anima" metaphors, and Reich the "orgone." The humanists talk about "peak experiences," while the mechanists deal with "little black boxes." Berne has "games," Perls has a "top dog" and an "under dog," Janov has "primal" experiences, and EST graduates presumably get "it."

Each therapy or system of psychology, then, has as one of its basic constituents a set of metaphors (in the form of a vocabulary) which for some individuals is capable of conveying some measure of what their experience of the world is like. An important distinction for us to make, however, is that these metaphors are *not* the experiences themselves. People do not contain within their heads and bodies little top dogs and primal beings running around looking for an IT to wrestle with. *Metaphors are a way of talking about experience.*

Suppose that you say to me, "My right arm feels like it's full of lead." I would certainly be missing the point if, upon hearing your statement, I were to begin beating your arm with a hammer in order to hear its metallic ring. Having an arm "full of lead" is a *verbal representation of an experience*—that is, a metaphor. The actual experience itself, however, is unavailable to anyone but the person having that experience. Using our example, one person may feel that his arm is "heavy," another may feel that it is "immobile," and still a third may feel that her arm is "dense." Although the experiences of each of these individuals is unique, they could all verbally express with equivalent accuracy their perceptions with the metaphorical phrase, "My arm feels like it's full of lead."

The point to be gained from this example is that whenever a native speaker of English makes a verbal communication, that communication is a metaphorical (and, thus, incomplete) representation of that person's actual experience.[1] The point to be *made* from the example is that when you, as a therapist or a conversationalist, construct and express to another person a "metaphor," that listener will take what he hears and *represent it in terms of his or her own experience.* Whenever we as human beings are presented with some kind of sensory, perceptual, or cognitive input, we consciously or unconsciously try to make sense out of that input. That is, we try to represent that input in a way that is meaningful to us as functioning, utilizing beings. If you have ever had your perceptions of the world altered by a drug, or if you have ever found yourself in a group of people whose language you did not speak, you probably know how important it is to "make sense" out of one's world.

The importance of the above discussion for anyone who acts either professionally or avocationally as a people-helper is for you to understand that when you as a people-helper listen to a client talk about his situation, he is presenting to you a set of metaphors which you make sense of as best you can. The "sense" you make of those metaphors can never, however, be identical with the actual experience of your client. Your response to the client will also be similarly "misunderstood" to some degree by him. Obviously, such a system of communication by metaphor can, and often does, lead to a great deal of miscommunication and confusion. In at least this one respect we are all regular guests at the Mad Hatter's tea parties.

What is the origin of these fundamental differences? Each human being develops for him or herself a *model of the world* based upon a combination of genetically determined factors and upon experience. A "model" includes all of the experiences, all of the generalizations related to those experiences, and all of the rules which govern the application of those generalizations. Imagine for a moment that you decide to drive to Terra Haute, Indiana and that upon seeing the Terra Haute city limit sign you turn off the road and drive right into that sign. That, of course, is an experience. After brushing yourself off, confessing to the policeman, and carefully analyzing the situation, you go on to make the generalization that "signs are not the things that they signify." Then from your experience and generalization you formulate the rule: DO NOT DRIVE INTO CITY LIMIT SIGNS. This is the same process you have used (perhaps since before birth) to build up an amazingly complex world model consisting of the sum-total of your experiences and the lessons you have generated from those experiences. Some parts of this model change along with physiological development and in response to new experiences, while other parts of the model seem rigid and unchangeable.

And, no two world models are alike. The data on thousands of experiments on perception and individual differences attest to the fact that there are significant differences between us all on a neuro-physiological level. If, for example, we show a line to a group of people then ask them to match it to one in a group of twenty lines of varying lengths, some of our observers will *consistently* match to lines which are too long. The same is true in identifying colors, distances, auditory tones, and so on. Of course these judgements are sufficiently close for most of us to agree that the clouds hanging in the blue sky at sunset are "reddish-orange". Yet the fact remains that we are each perceiving slightly different hues. Beyond subtle neuro-physiological differences there is the perhaps more profound shaping effect of the variety of our individual experiences. Even identical twins raised side-by-side will at least occasionally be treated by Chance to differing experiences. And so we all evolve our own unique models of the world. This is an important distinction to make, since gathering accurate information is basic to any effective therapeutic situation. By understanding that all communication is metaphorical and based on unique experience we alert ourselves to the fact that it is therefore also incomplete and that it is the *listener* who fills in the holes.

Of course, there are not only differences between models, but many similarities as well. These similarities are partially the result of being raised within similar social milieus. The similarities that will be of greatest use to us in developing and utilizing therapeutic metaphors are those which describe patterns of *how* people communicate their experience of the world. It is with these patterns that this book is concerned.

SECTION 2
Helping People With Metaphors

As we saw above, unconsciously, and on a very basic level, people-helpers have always used metaphor as an important part of the process of therapy. When a client comes asking for help with some "problems," he also comes with a unique model of the world. That is, the client has developed for himself specific ideas as to what constitutes the experiences of love, hate, generosity, happiness, interest, city limit signs, and so on. Although members of our culture usually agree on the general characteristics of each of these experiences, the actual *experiencing* of them is unique for each individual. A primary focus of therapy has always been the attempt of the therapist to understand the client's model of the world. Towards this end, the therapist asks the client to describe in detail his experiences regarding the problem under discussion. The underlying assumption is that if the therapist is going to help the client change the therapist must first understand how the client presently sees, hears, and grasps the world.

Metaphors are an important part of this information-gathering process. Each metaphorical piece of information presented by the client is understood and interpreted by the therapist in terms of his own model of the world. Frequently, the therapist will check out his interpretation with that of the client's so as to be sure that they are talking about the same thing. For example:

Joe: And so my wife mopes around all the time.

Therapist: You mean she looks sad and listless?

Joe: Oh no, she looks okay. It's just that everything she says is so pessimistic.

Had the therapist in the above example not checked out his model with that of the client's he would have drawn conclusions about Joe's wife which, though plausible, were completely incorrect. Joe's wife is not "listless," but "pessimistic"—two very different things. Hopefully, this process of distillation ultimately results in the therapist commanding a sufficiently complete and *accurate* "map" of the client's situation and experience of that situation.

Very often this process of model distillation includes the beginnings of therapeutic change. As the client expresses himself, he sometimes encounters aspects of his experience for which he "has no words." For example:

Joe: And when she's like that, I just feel, uh, bad.

Therapist: 'Bad' in what way?

Joe: Oh, I don't know. Just, you know, bad!

Therapist: Depressed, lonely, angry, . . .?

Joe: Lonely, that's it. Lonely.

In this example, the therapist has assisted Joe in recovering for himself a one-word *metaphorical* description of how he experiences a particular event. That is, Joe feels "loneliness" when his wife is "like that." Remember that Joe's experience of "loneliness" is as yet very unspecified, since he has not yet described what "loneliness" entails for him (that is, "loneliness" *is* not being with whom, in what ways, and for how long?). However, since "loneliness" is a member of a *class* of feelings considered by Joe to be BAD, it *is* more specific than "bad," closer to Joe's actual experience, and so of more use in understanding Joe's model of the world.

Another possibility is that Joe might be having difficulty adequately describing certain *areas* of his experience:

Therapist: How are you 'lonely' when she's like that?

Joe: Well, it's just like I feel she's not . . . I don't know. Involved, I guess. (Joe shakes his head and is clearly confused.)

Therapist: Like being involved in a game and she doesn't want to play?

Joe: Uh, no, not really . . .

Therapist: Perhaps like working on a project together and she wants you to do it all?

Joe: Yeah. That's more like it. She cares what happens alright, but she wants me to do everything.

Again the therapist has assisted Joe in specifying his actual experience in terms of a metaphor which is relatively comprehensive and satisfying for him. *Most importantly, this new and more complete metaphorical representation provides both Joe and his therapist with a mutually understandable way of talking about Joe's problem.* Within the implications of the metaphor— "working on a project"— they can be relatively sure that they will be talking about the same experience.

Suppose for a moment that the therapist knows nothing about differing world-models and the metaphors which connect them. All of the processes we have briefly discussed so far are tools which we, as language users, use every time we communicate with another individual. And, like any tool, when not used properly they become potential (even if unintentional) weapons. This unintentional misuse can occur at the most basic levels of communication. For instance, a therapist and Joe may be using the same word, but neither realizes or considers that they are *not* representing the same experience by that word. Not only is the therapist limiting himself in terms of communicating with Joe (i.e., understanding Joe's model of the world), but, using his inaccurate model as a guide, the therapist may then attempt to "help" Joe. Since the therapist is operating out of a faulty model (as far as Joe is concerned), he is likely to make therapeutic interpretations, suggestions, and strategy decisions which are inappropriate for Joe's particular situation. Such "therapeutic interventions" could even be detrimental.

Suppose that, in the above transcript excerpt, Joe's therapist had no awareness of, or appreciation for, the fact that no two world models are alike. Their interchange might then have been quite different:

Joe: And so my wife just mopes around.

Therapist: Do you know why?

Joe: No, I don't. I've been trying and trying to figure it out, but I can't.

Therapist: Is she angry with you about anything?

Joe: Not that I know of.

Therapist: Have you asked?

Joe: Oh sure. And she says that I'm a model husband. That I take care of her real well.

Therapist: Well, have you tried doing some special things for her, like taking the kids off her hands so she could get out of the house?

Joe: No, I haven't done that. . .I guess I could try it though.

You will no doubt recognize the communication patterns in this transcript excerpt as ones which commonly occur in the realm of people-helping. As we know from before, Joe's experience of his wife's "moping" has to do with her reaction to his having (being given?) most of the responsibility for care of the family. Her reaction is to be pessimistic about various aspects of the family. On the other hand, the experience that the therapist derives from his own world-model of the metaphor MOPE involves being "secretively angry" about something, and in need of "more freedom from responsibilities." Operating from this inaccurate (for Joe) representation, the therapist attempts to get Joe to grasp the experience in terms of the therapist's model. The therapist ends up suggesting that Joe try certain changes which, as we already know, would facilitate precisely what his wife does not want to happen. At worst, our therapist's unintentional ignorance could magnify Joe's problem. At best, valuable therapeutic time has been spent in miscommunication. This therapist no doubt had only good intentions in mind when he made his suggestions to Joe. The fact is, though, that this therapist was not equipped at that time to appropriately act upon his intentions—no matter how good. If so much miscommunication can result from ignoring the world-model differences between two individuals for one word, you can readily see that such ignorance applied to the world-models being described in sentences and in collections of sentences will geometrically increase the number of miscommunications involved. The problem of *completely* understanding a communication made by another person would seem to be impossible to overcome. It is impossible. . . for, in order to do that, you would have to be that person at the same time he or she was communicating with you.

Fortunately, that level of communication is not necessary in order to help another change. (However, a great deal towards achieving that level of communication is possible merely by recognizing that *your model of the world is necessarily different from that of any other human being's.*)

The Transderivational Search

Perhaps the most important concept for you to understand as an individual using metaphors is that of the "transderivational search." In the previous section we saw that each of us enjoys a unique model of the world—a model which your personal experience has, over time, tailored to suite you and you alone. This model of yours is comprised of all of your stored experiences and the generalizations you have made about those experiences. It is with this model that all incoming sensory information is compared and correlated. Sensory information which "fits" with the model "makes sense" (literally), while sensory information which is totally new or contradictory "does not make sense."

For example: I have a foreign car (a Peugeot) in which the door-locking buttons are pulled *up* to lock and pushed *down* to unlock the doors (which is, of course, contrary to the system used on all American automobiles). A friend of mine approached my car with the object of getting in, noticed that the locking button was up, and, with the confidence of thousands of experiences with car doors to back him up, vainly tried to open the door. He finally resigned and gave me "the bad news" that my door was "broken." He was, in fact, so secure in his own world model regarding car doors that he never once tried pushing the locking button down, even though the window was completely open during this entire episode.

This example is instructive on several levels. First of all, it illustrates how having a set model of the world can be both a help and a hinderance. The advantage of our relatively stable world models is that they free us from continually testing and retesting our environment (that is, you do not have to figure out how car doors work every time you encounter one). The disadvantage is that a *set* world model is relatively inflexible and, so, limiting (as we saw in the above anecdote—after all, had I not intervened, he might never have made it into the car).

Secondly, the story illustrates the tremendous power that our individual models can exert on our behavior. When an experience has been repeated many times and/or has been profound in its effects it generates rules about the world which can be tremendously compelling. Many times the effect is so strong that a person faced with an experience which is contradictory to his model will wholly or in part delete from his awareness the inconsistent experience. From the point of view of the person, the inconsistency of an experience ceases to be a problem when the experience ceases to be seen, felt, and heard. More often, as in the anecdote, the inconsistent experience is seen from another perspective so as to resolve the contradiction in a manner acceptable to the individual's model of the world. (It was not that door locks could be different or that his present or past perceptions could be wrong—it was *my* door that was "broken.")

The third important point made by the anecdote is found in the process my friend used to make sense out of the paradox with which he was confronted. In going back through his experiences with car doors he retrieved the information that an "up" button meant that the door was unlocked. When the door did not open he was forced to somehow understand what was going on, and to do this he again *went back through* his world model until he could identify a part of it which "made sense" out of his experience— that the door was "broken." This process of going back through our world models in order to make sense out of our experiences is called the *transderivational search*. The way in which you understand the words you are reading here is by relating them (via transderivational searches) to appropriate parts of your model. If you see the letters DOG you initiate a transderivational search for the past experience(s) with which you can correlate the letters DOG. That is how you know what DOG "means." And as you already know from our previous discussions, the pictures, feelings, sounds, and smells that each one of us conjures up out of our models in response to DOG will be unique in many ways.

It is precisely this process of correlating sensory input with one's world model that makes metaphors so powerful as agents of change. When as a therapist you or I relate to a client any story, that person will initiate transderivational searches in order to make sense out of what is being said. Furthermore, since the context within which the story is being told is a "therapy session" the client (who, it must be remembered, is *seeking* alleviation of some kind of "pain") is likely to correlate as much as possible what is being said with his own problem-situation.

The fairy tale is therapeutic because the patient finds his *own* solutions, through contemplating what the story seems to imply about him and his inner conflicts at this moment in his life. The content of the chosen tale usually has nothing to do with the patient's external life, but much to do with his inner problems, which seem incomprehensible and hence unsolvable. The fairy tale clearly does not refer to the outer world, although it may begin realistically enough and have everyday features woven into it. The unrealistic nature of these tales (which narrow-minded rationalists object to) is an important device, because it makes obvious that the fairy tales' concern is not useful information about the external world, but the inner processes taking place in an individual.

(from *The Uses of Enchantment* by Bettelheim, page 25)

As you will learn in the pages to come, the purpose of therapeutic metaphors is to initiate either conscious or unconscious transderivational searches which will assist a person in gaining for himself the personal resources and enhanced world model he needs in order to be able to handle the problem with which he is grappling. What, then, is the nature of metaphors which will allow us to achieve these goals?

Formal Metaphors

Metaphors, in the form of fairytales, parables, and anecdotes, are consciously and unconsciously used by therapists in order to assist a client in making the changes he wants to make. A client may express some area of experience where he feels limited in viable choices, or perhaps sees no alternatives whatever. At this point, occasionally the therapist will tell an anecdote out of his own experience, that of another client, or merely invent one. The hope underlying this story-telling is that the experiences of another in overcoming a problem which is similar to that of the client's will suggest to him directly or indirectly ways in which he can deal with the situation. Going back to Joe and the therapist, the therapist could launch into a story about a previous client who had a problem similar to Joe's. In the course of his narrative, the therapist develops in what ways Joe's problem is similar to this "other client's problem." The difference, however, is that this "other client's problem" has a *resolution* of some kind. Hearing this, Joe can, if it fits his model of the world, incorporate that resolution into his own situation. If the story's resolution does not fit for him, he will at least know that a resolution is possible and perhaps begin searching for one (for many therapists, this is often the primary "reason" for relating such anecdotes).

The most important requirement for an effective metaphor is that it *meet the client at his model of the world.* That does *not* mean that the content of the metaphor is necessarily the same as that of the client's situation. "Meeting the client at his model of the world" means that the metaphor preserves the *structure* of the client's problematic situation. That is, the significant factors in the metaphor are the client's interpersonal *relationships* and *patterns* of coping within the context of the "problem." The context itself is *not* important. For example, we might tell Joe the following anecdote. . . .

> You know, Joe, I had a friend in college who was very good at writing lab reports. He had a lovely girlfriend who was also a science major. Consequently they were in many classes together. Naturally, they paired-up in order to write their lab reports. . .which he enjoyed—except for one thing. For some reason, his girlfriend felt that she wasn't competent enough to write lab reports. So she kind of sat back and let him write them while she looked on. This was okay with him at first, but soon he got tired of doing all the work, and, more importantly, he realized that she was missing out on opportunities to broaden her horizons, in the sense of learning new skills. He got an idea one day that really worked well. While they were working on a lab report, he pretended to be at a loss for

words in describing the set-up. He was so completely stopped that she very quickly told him the
obvious words needed to complete the sentence.
He thanked her for her help and kissed her warmly.
Soon, however, he was again 'stumped.' Again she
helped him out, and so it went until he was finally
able to turn over to her whole sections of the lab
report to do on her own. The next time they did
a lab, she actually demanded her fair share of it,
and, my friend, he was of course very happy to
share it with her.

This anecdote is only one of an infinite number of equivalently
meaningful and effective metaphors that could have been constructed. If you take a moment to go back over the few short conversations we have had with Joe about his relationship with his
wife, you will see the parallels between what is occuring within
their relationship and within that of the "friends" in the anecdote.
Those two "friends" could just as easily have been a king whose
queen would not help him rule, a stallion whose mare would not
help pull the wagon, or one side of a triumphal arch, the other
side of which is crumbling. As long as the metaphor and Joe's
problem are structurally similar, he will unconsciously and perhaps
consciously correlate them.[2] What is significant about Joe's metaphor is that *it preserves within it the relationships and coping
patterns which operate in the "real" problem, and that it provides
a solution to the problem.* Because those patterns which characterize Joe's problem are preserved in the structure of the anecdote
he will, via transderivational searches, make for himself meaning
out of the story's events in terms of his own problem situation.
Once identified (either consciously or unconsciously) with the
story line, Joe is free to incorporate and utilize (or reject) the
resolution offered.

In the chapters to follow you will be presented with explicit
models of the patterns which are important in the formation of
therapeutic metaphors so that those of you who wish to assist
others in expanding their models of the world (making the changes
they want to make) will be able to develop for yourselves skills

which will allow you to formulate and effectively use therapeutic metaphors. Regardless of whether one is tailoring for the client an anecdote involving an actual occurrence or one is spontaneously inventing a suitable fairytale, if the patterns which are explained in the following chapters are applied to the construction and presentation of those metaphors they will become more relevant, intelligible, and effective as agents of change.

Effective Metaphors

Constructing effective metaphors is not *necessarily* contingent upon being able to incorporate all of the metaphor-building tools described in the pages to come. A metaphor which satisfies the basic pattern requirement of being structurally equivalent with the problem situation and providing a workable resolution can be not only therapeutically effective, *it may also be sufficient.* All of the many patterns of communication and experience which you will be learning about here are not necessary to communicate to another person the "message" contained in the anecdote. However, with each of those model distinctions that you *do* add, you will increase the significance, resolution, and thoroughness of your metaphorical interventions.

By *significance* we are referring to the client's conscious or unconscious experience of similarity between his own situation and that portrayed in the metaphor. Structural equivalence alone insures a degree of similarity, but, depending upon the obviousness (to the client) of the metaphor, it may also make the metaphor vulnerable to "resistance" by the client (this is more fully discussed in Part VI). However, the patterns of communication described in Parts III, IV, and V are beyond the conscious awareness of most individuals, and so are irresistable in terms of their significance. Consider the following example:

> A woman client is being told a tale directed at helping her curtail her activities as the neighborhood busybody. She is aware that she is a snoop,

> but she is not aware that she also *blames* others frequently and that she represents most of her experience *visually*. Part of the tale told to her runs like this (these additional levels of communication are identified for you by *italics*). . .

> Therapist: And in this forest community there lived an anteater named Wag. Now Wag, of course, had a long nose. This didn't bother her, but she could *see* that it was often the *focus* of attention in the forest, which did sometimes bother her. When a squirrel came up to admire her snout she *narrowed her eyes* at it and *haughtily* said, *"Isn't it obvious that you should* be nut-gathering now, instead of this wool-gathering?" . . . .

Now, in our example, it is very likely that the client will recognize the metaphorical connections between her being a busybody and Wag's nose. If she consequently takes offense to, or is bored with, the obviousness of the story connections she may jeopardize this therapeutic opportunity by that time-honored game of "Staying One Jump Ahead of the Therapist." If, however, the story is simultaneously operating on *other* unconscious, parallel, and equally indicative levels of communication, then the metaphor remains irresistible in its significance for the client.

The increase in *resolution* referred to above is the result of the increase in character and process distinctions that automatically occurs with the addition of each of the metaphor-building tools. Each of those tools contributes detail to the story, and in so doing creates a fuller, more completely equivalent representation of the actual problem situation.

The third advantage of including some or all of the model-building distinctions is that of *thoroughness*. Whenever an individual experiences a "problem," that problem is represented at many different levels of conscious and unconscious awareness and behavior.

PROBLEM
EXPERIENCE
$\left\{\begin{array}{l}\text{People Involved (Part II)}\\\text{Dynamics of the Situation (Part II)}\\\text{Linguistic Patterns (Part II)}\\\text{Communication Modes (Part III)}\\\text{Representational System Patterns (Part IV)}\\\text{Sub-Modality Patterns (Part V)}\end{array}\right.$

When we try to help others (or ourselves) change, we usually make those changes on one or two of the most apparent levels at which our experience is represented. For instance, a self-effacing man who can't relax with his lover could find another lover with whom he feels more comfortable. Another choice he has is to change the way in which he communicates from self-effacing to, perhaps, blaming (which would naturally result in changes in his relationship with his lover). In either case, he (and we) trust that changes at one level will generalize throughout the other levels. Sometimes this trust is justified, and sometimes no matter what change is made "that same old problem is still there." One excellent way to insure that the metaphorical work you are doing is effective in promoting change is to be thorough—which means providing for all of the necessary changes in the various problem levels within the metaphor. By tying-up all of the loose ends at once you will avoid running the risk of them tripping you up later on.

If you are thinking that handling that many loose ends is an awesome task, I agree with you. But it is also like learning any other skill—awesome at first, practiced, then easily performed by a cooperative combination of conscious and unconscious creativity and experience. You once sat at a small wooden desk diligently copying onto funny paper with wide lines the letters and words your teacher printed on the blackboard before you. The reward of that practice is that now you can take pen in hand and flow onto a page streams of words without ever having to consciously think about the necessity to dot "i"s and cross "t"s. It is suggested that in acquiring the ability to spontaneously create and use therapeutic metaphors you first practice building them using only the basic concept of structural equivalence. You will find that your ability to create metaphors which effectively match the problem situations of your clients soon becomes effortless and automatic. At that point begin adding to your repertoire each of the other levels of communication described in this book. With practice you will discover that you can gather all of the necessary information about the client's situation and then, with little conscious effort, invent a metaphor which is structurally similar, offers a resolution, *and* includes all of the other communication patterns as well.

Natural Metaphors

This is probably a good point at which to draw your attention to the fact that those components which combine to create an effective therapeutic metaphor are components which very often occur as the natural and unconscious result of story-telling. In making up a tale we more often than not unconsciously construct it so that it correlates with some personal or shared experiences, provide a resolution, include various levels of significance, and tell it in such a way as to maximize transderivational searching in our listeners.

As an illustration of this naturally occurring process, following is a fairytale which was told to a friend of mine by her older brother. Despite the fact that her brother had no formal knowledge of metaphors his impromptu fairytale exhibits virtually all of the elements of a complete therapeutic metaphor. (After you have read Parts II, III, IV, and V, return to this short tale and read it again—your time will be richly rewarded.)

Once upon a time, in the far distant land of Nod, there lived a troll who guarded the bridge between the townsfolk of Nod and the dwellers of the Rollin' Hills . . . . Now this troll was the only living being who had direct contact with both the townspeople, who were nicknamed "normals" and the hills people, or the "primitives." Both the normals and the primitives knew of each other, the normals having a long history of folk lore which spoke of those mysterious and boisterous little folk who hid by day and frolicked in the star and moon light. The normals had always considered the hillspeople to be of a lower class than themselves, for the primitives loved to frolick and play with moonbeams, hurling them from the hills down into the town, and yowling and stomping while the more sedate normals were trying to get their eight hours in order to function at their maximum capacity during the day. The normals main pleasure was to realize that they had the stamina and capability to function as a unit in order to be the most efficient town in Nod. So you see, the normals considered the primitives with far from friendly feelings . . . you might even say they were a pain in the ass, you just might say, I'm not sure though, if you will or not . . . . The primitives, too, had very lengthy accounts of the townspeople and considered them to be very dull. They were different from the townsfolk, though, in that they had been raised in the tradition of confronting the townspeople. . . , yet the methods which they used seemed of no avail and the primitives called a Pit meeting to settle the problem, for they wished the normals to experience their side of life, which they felt was definitely more fun . . . . During the Pit meeting, the first ever called, they sang and danced and ate and had a jolly good time. To their surprise, however, no conclusions had been made, or even arisen. Life continued along it's way until one day, at twilight—just before the normals were fixin' for bed and the primitives getting up and washing their long beards in preparation for the evening . . . a strange sound was heard. All the inhabitants of the town and the hill froze in their tracks.

Where was that sound coming from? Slowly, as they listened, they began to distinguish the voice of the troll . . . it was a forlorn sound, coming from the valley between the two peoples. It sounded like the low rumble of a dying dragon. Seeing as how the primitives had known and been friendly with the troll, they were concerned and went over to see what was wrong. The townspeople too heard the sounds and were startled from their beds . . . they too went to the bridge. And so, in the twilight hour on this evening, under the darkening sky were gathered both the primitives and the normals, with the troll in between. And the troll began speaking . . . "I have witnessed the communication between you two for years, and years . . . longer than I can remember; and now the time has come. You both have your own ways of dealing with life, and for each of you, your way is the right way at this point in time."

The primatives looked at the normals, and the normals looked at the primatives and they knew that he was right; and just at that moment, the normals began to laugh, and the primatives were awed to silence . . . .

And so began a new age, the primatives and normals sharing their ways of life.

SECTION 3
Plan of the Book

Each of the following Parts will give you explicit tools with which to fashion effective therapeutic metaphors. Part II describes the basic metaphor model and patterns for effective delivery. Part III, Part IV, and Part V explain Satir categories, representational systems, and sub-modalities respectively. At the end of Part II is a metaphor (fairytale) which, at the end of each of Parts III, IV, and V, is repeated, adding to it—one at a time—each of the three patterns of communication described. Ways of utilizing metaphors are discussed in Part VI.

The plan of the book is that it be used as a *workbook*. So, I recommend that you read it through once, then re-read it a Part at a time. After reading each Part for the second time, experiment until you are comfortable with using the concepts presented. And then move on to the next Part. The book has been organized into bite sized chunks so that you can easily digest them. Also, scattered throughout the book are short and simple exercises designed to provide you with better understandings and some experience handling the model.

In order to provide you with a reference structure for the rest of the book, following is a complete therapeutic metaphor, which also appears in annotated form in Part VII.

Vivace's Metaphor

In a place not unlike this place, there lived a man and his two daughters. He was a very intelligent man who took great pride in his daughters and provided for them as best he could. They lived in a small house in the forest.

His two daughters were named Let and Ho. As youngsters, Let and Ho shared all of their adventures. Each day they would rush out to the forest to make their little discoveries. They made little people out of pine cones, and play houses with trees for walls and a sky for a roof. Of course they also saw, and regularly conversed with, all manner of elves, leprachauns, and fairies. And when they were hungry, it didn't take them long to hunt-up a bush full of their favorite berries. When they were ready, they would return home, run up to Father and hug him tightly. He hugged them back, laughed, and sat down on his knee, ready to listen to the particulars of their day's wanderings. He was always fascinated by their adventures, for although he was scholarly, in many ways he was not in touch with the world. He rarely roamed from home, and often wondered what it was like out in the forest.

And so it went, year after year. Let and Ho grew together, dropping off worn-out games and replacing them with new ones.

Then one day Father fell unforeseeably and unaccountably blind. Over the time that followed, Let and Ho also began to change. Let continued to spend most of her day romping in the forest. She loved to feel the cool air on her face as she ran, the low branches stinging her legs. She never tired of stroking the furry tufts of green pine needles, or running her hands over the rough bark of the trees. When she would come upon a berry bush, Let would sometimes take a handful and crush them just because it was such an interesting sensation. And when she was tired, she would lay down on a mossy hillside or on a springy carpet of pine needles.

Ho, on the other hand, saw her place as being in the home. She loved the forest no less than before, and enjoyed gazing at it from the house. She particularly appreciated the blending of colors and shadows as they changed through the day and year. She knew, however, that her greatest pleasure came when she was focusing her attention on the household and its needs. She loved to cook. There was always something special for her about watching a bunch of ingredients combine, disappear into the oven, and emerge obviously changed. Ho also had a talent for seeing what had to be done around the house, and so it was always a picture of orderliness. And, of course, she assumed most of the responsibility for watching out for Father.

Time went on. Often Ho and Let had little to do with one another. And in some ways they got along, and in some ways they didn't. Let would sometimes say to Ho, "You shouldn't spend so much time at home. Why can't you drop that stuff for awhile? And besides, you shouldn't be tending Father so much. He can take care of himself, you know."

Ho would then reply, "I just know Father needs someone there to watch over him. And I don't mind, really. I like what I do here, and if only you didn't worry about me then everything would be perfect." Even so, once in awhile Ho would feel stirring within her the need to fly into the forest. But since her duties were clearly at home, she would dim those stirrings as best she could.

One day a young man stepped out of the forest and up to the house. Ho saw him first and invited him in. He explained that he was on a journey which, as far as he knew, would never end. And, although Let often pressed him for information, he was quite secretive in many ways. Father, Let, and Ho understood his position, and asked no further questions about his past. The young man asked to stay for awhile in exchange for doing needed chores and repairs. They all agreed.

Not long after the young man had arrived, he came bounding out of the forest calling for Ho. She saw that he was out of breath, and asked him what was the matter.

"Ah," he said, "Ho, I need your help for something that is quite important to us all. Will you see your way clear to join me?"

Ho agreed, and together they set off through the forest. Along the way he said, "We will also need the help of Let. Let's call her."

Using her loudest voice, Ho joined the young man in calling out Let's name. Soon they heard a crashing of underbrush, which was soon followed by Let, picking her way through the bushes. She joined them in their search.

After going a ways, the young man stopped them and said, "We are here."

They were standing a short distance away from the edge of a large ravine. The bottom of the ravine was thickly forested. The forest from which they had just emerged ended a number of feet from the edge of the ravine, creating a barren strip of ground that completely ringed the perimeter of the ravine.

"But where are we?" both Let and Ho chimed in together.

The young man looked wistful and said, "Well, I will tell you. When I was somewhat younger, I met a man on the road. We struck up a conversation and decided to travel together for awhile. At one point he removed his hat just long enough for me to get a glimpse of his ears. They were a strange color! When I asked him about his ears he confessed that he was a sorcerer. After a moment of confusion I asked him, 'Now that I know that you're a sorcerer, does that mean you won't travel further with me?' It turned out that he was afraid I wouldn't want to stay with *him*! He was very relieved, so we journeyed together until our crossroads. As a parting gift, he told me about a special orchard that produced all manner of strange and delicious fruits. He explained that it was not possible to describe where it was to be found, but did tell me how I would know *when* I had found it."

"How?" both girls whispered.

"A special feeling . . . and I know it's around here."

The three of them then began to search all over for the orchard. Let soon tired and sat down to unknot her hair. Meanwhile, Ho continued to scan, looking for a sign. She walked carefully to the edge of the ravine . . . and peered intently at its forested floor.

Then she saw it.

Down in the trees, through a small opening in the leaves, she saw the sunlight reflected off of a colored surface. As she looked closer, she could see by the way in which the light played upon that surface that it was smooth, curved to make a sphere, and it was hard . . . and definitely worth going after. Now she also noticed that it was a very warm, deep red. She felt tingly inside as she watched a beam of light fall there.

"There it is," she said in a calm voice as she pointed into the ravine. Let and the young man followed her pointing finger until they too saw it.

"You've found it," he whispered, and he gently pinched her right cheek. "Now, how will we reach it?" All three stood on the brink of the ravine and looked down at the steep walls which appeared to surround it. Ho spent some time looking over the steep walls, checking for a path or entrance. But she soon got eyestrain, and so she sat down on the ledge and dangled her feet.

Finally, Let knew what she had to do. "I'll get down there," she intoned. With that she lowered herself over the edge. She felt carefully with her feet for whatever footholds she could find. At the same time she grasped with her hands what secure stones or roots were within reach. She made her way down a few feet, then ran out of places to place her feet. She slipped a few times. It was then that she looked down at her feet. As she gazed at the area around them, she noticed that by looking for the shadows she could clearly identify likely crevices and footholds. Consequently she was able to continue with considerable ease. At one point she called up to the others waiting at the ledge:

"Watch me closely," she yelled, "and it will be easy for you to follow!" It was then that the young man winked at her with his left eye.

He and Ho carefully watched all of the graceful movements that Let used, and soon they too were nimbly climbing down into the ravine.

In the ravine they scattered about, chattering like a flock of birds. Then they came upon the special orchard. And it was indeed special. All manner of strange trees and bushes grew there. And from each there was hanging myriads of exotically shaped and colored fruits. Some even changed shape or color as they were handled. Each had a special texture to its skin. Some went from being rough to being smooth when gently squeezed. There were dense ones and fluffy ones, both large and small. When you shook this one, it rattled. When you plucked that one, it "popped." And still another made the most pleasant crackling sound when it was opened. All day they spent in tasting and experimenting with the fruits. Many were delightfully delicious and satisfying. Some were quite bitter, but they rapidly discovered that the bitter ones had many other uses. A most remarkable orchard.

Each day they would return to the orchard. And each time they descended or ascended the ravine wall they would make their trail a little more worn, until they were soon walking a pleasant path to their special place. Once in the orchard, they would enjoy wonderful conversations in which they discovered much about one another. Ho found that her walks into the forest were so relaxing and invigorating that taking care of the house became easier and more enjoyable. And Let soon began to see ways in which she could bring the things she had learned about the forest into their home, and in that way became a vital part of them both.

One day Ho and Let awoke to discover that the young man had gone. They didn't fret, for they had always known that he would someday leave .... They had always known that the orchard they had found wasn't his orchard.

And so, together, Let and Ho continued their trips of comfort and discovery to their orchard.

One morning Father said, "Well, it's long overdue, but certainly not too late. Daughters, be so kind as to show me the way to that orchard." Ho took him by the right hand, and Let took him by the left. Together they led him through the forest, all of them talking gaily as they went. When they reached the ravine, Father said, "Let me go for a moment . . . there is something I must find out for myself."

Father then took small steps toward the brink of the ravine. When he reached the edge he dangled one of his feet over into the emptiness, and smiled.

"I always wondered," he said. "If you ladies will take my hands now, I'm ready to visit this orchard of yours."

They led him down the path. When they reached the bottom, Father spoke again. "Leave me be now. I'll find it on my own." Let and Ho were worried about him at first, but after talking it over they decided that it was important. So while they sat in the orchard, Father meandered about the ravine floor. Sometimes he smacked up against a tree. Sometimes he tripped and fell. Let and Ho always knew where he was, because they could hear him giggling to, and about, himself.

Father at last *did* find the orchard, and he spent the afternoon wandering from plant to plant, tasting whatever he could. Let and Ho felt very pleased and so at ease that they soon forgot about Father (who was, at that point, not in the least interested in being remembered). Instead Let and

Ho continued to dream their dreams and discuss their hopes.

And so it went. They returned to the Little orchard whenever they needed to and whenever they wanted to. And sometimes that was often. And sometimes it was not. But they always knew that it was there . . . .

FOOTNOTES TO PART I

1. We are here using the concept "metaphor" to include the notion that words themselves are representations of ("stand for") experience—they are not the experiences themselves. This understanding of metaphors is not crucial for making and using therapeutic metaphors, but it is important for an understanding of therapeutic communication in general and sub-modalities in particular (Part V). For an expanded discussion of this use of "metaphor," see Collin Turbayne's *The Myth of Metaphor*, Yale University Press, 1962.

2. In Part VI on Utilization we will take up a more extensive discussion of conscious and unconscious learning through metaphor. For now, it is sufficient to observe that as human beings we often come to "learn," "understand," or "know" things without being consciously aware of when, where, or how we came to know them. For an excellent discussion of the nature of unconscious communication and learning see Volumes I, 2, and 3 of *Patterns of the Hypnotic Techniques of Milton H. Erickson, M.D.* by Bandler, Grinder, and DeLozier.

PART II
BUILDING YOUR METAPHOR

PROLOGUE

"That Old Time Feeling"

Song by Guy Clark

That old time feelin' goes sneakin' down
    the hall
Like an old grey cat in winter keepin'
    close to the wall
And that old time feelin' comes stumblin'
    up the street
Like an old salesman kickin' the papers
    from his feet
That old time feelin' draws circles round
    the block
Like old women with no children holdin'
    hands with the clock
And that old time feelin' falls on its face
    in the park
Like an old wino prayin' he can make it
    till it's dark
That old time feelin' comes and goes in
    the rain
Like an old man with his checkers dyin'
    to find a game
And that old time feelin' plays for beer in
    bars
Like an old bluestime picker who don't recall
    who you are
That old time feelin' limps through the
    night on a crutch
Like an old soldier wonderin' if he's paid
    too much

And that old time feelin' rocks and spits
    and cries
Like an old lover rememberin' the girl
    with the clear blue eyes
That old time feelin' goes sneakin' down
    the hall
Like an old grey cat in winter keepin'
    close to the wall

BUILDING YOUR METAPHOR

SECTION 1
Well-Formedness

Therapeutic metaphors, like therapies in general, begin with THE PROBLEM. The first major task for a people-helper is to gain some kind of understanding about the nature and characteristics of the problem, and in what ways the client wants to change his situation. Much of what is important in gathering such information was discussed in Part I.[1] One vital aspect of establishing the PROBLEM is often overlooked, however, and has consequently hindered or scuttled many therapeutic encounters. That aspect is the *well-formedness* of the problem.

> A woman in an airport had just missed her plane, which by that time was airborne. She went stomping up to the desk of the airline, raved that she *had* to be on that (now departed) flight, and loudly demanded that they bring the plane back for her. Hoping to appease her, the airline representative told her that he would see what he could do. She was obviously pleased and expecting "action," and he was just as obviously lying in order to quiet her down. A few minutes later the representative returned, commiserated with the woman, assured her that it was not possible to bring back the flight, offered to help her arrange for another. . .then got hit with a purse.

Few people would disagree that this woman did have a problem and that the representative probably did want to help her. Their relationship was bound for disaster, however, because she had set a relatively impossible goal as the solution to her problem, and the representative at first tacitly accepted that goal. Her problem, then, was *ill-formed* in that its solution involved events and/or people over which neither she nor the representative had control. The same situation frequently occurs in the context of therapy. The client wants you to "make more days in the week," "make Jeff leave me alone," or "make Margaret love me." Although such requests for help represent for the client desirable outcomes, they are also beyond the control of the therapist, and so are candidates for long and fruitless therapy.

It is not that such therapeutic goals are "impossible," since they may in fact be realized. But, if they are, it is likely that that will be due to personal changes the *client* has made. *An important prerequiste of effective therapy and therapeutic metaphors, then, is that the client's goals be Well-Formed; that is, that the changes to be made are changes over which the client has control.* There is really no need for a therapist to get hit with a purse.

SECTION 2
Isomorphism

The fundamental characteristic of a therapeutic metaphor is that the characters and events which occur in the story are equivalent—*isomorphic*—with those individuals and events which characterize the client's situation or problem. Thus, each person significantly involved in the client's problem is represented in the metaphor's cast of characters. Similarly, the parameters of the situation and processes involved are also represented. These representations are *not* "equal" to the parameters of the problem, but are "equivalent" in the sense of maintaining the same *relationships* among the parameters in the metaphor as those found in the actual situation. For our purposes, then, "isomorphism" is the metaphorical preservation of the relationships occurring in the actual problem situation.

	Actual Situation		Metaphor
Significant Persons	Client ——— (Becomes) ⟶ X_c Person 1 ——— (Becomes) ⟶ Y_{p1} Person 2 ——— (Becomes) ⟶ Z_{p2}		Story Characters
Progression of Problem	Event 1 ——— (Becomes) ⟶ $Incident_{e1}$ Event 2 ——— (Becomes) ⟶ $Incident_{e2}$ Event 3 ——— (Becomes) ⟶ $Incident_{e3}$		Story Structure

In constructing an effective metaphor it is not sufficient to merely include in the story one character for each actual participant, and one story-line incident for each actual event. The relationships and sequencing of the actual situation must be preserved in the story in order for the client to accept it as a significant representation of his problem. This constraint means that what is significant about a metaphor is that it ismorphically represents the relationships and processes found in the problem. Therefore, *any context* is suitable as the setting for a metaphor provided that the constraint of isomorphism is satisfied.

In selecting characters for a metaphor it is of no consequence what they are—all that matters is *how they are related*. Suppose, for example, the problem involves a head-of-household father, a mother, and their young son, and that you choose a "boat" as a context for your story. One possibility for an isomorphic transformation of "the family" into "the protagonists" would be:

Significant Persons	Metaphor
Father ⟶	Captain
Mother ⟶	1st Mate
Son ⟶	Cabin Boy

In the example, the characters in the metaphor share many of the same logical (and even linguistic) relationships as do the actual family members. This same transformation can also be done for the significant events underlying their problem. The complete set of transformations might be something like the following:

Actual Situation		Metaphor
Father	—————— (Becomes) —————→	Captain
Mother	—————— (Becomes) —————→	1st Mate
Son	—————— (Becomes) —————→	Cabin Boy
family	—————— (Becomes) —————→	boat crew
father rarely home ↓	—————— (Becomes) —————→	captain often shut-up in cabin ↓
son gets into trouble ↓	—————— (Becomes) —————→	cabin boy sets the wrong sails ↓
mother covers for son ↓	—————— (Becomes) —————→	1st mate corrects him and tries to reset sails before captain sees ↓
father finds out, becomes furious, and leaves ↓	—————— (Becomes) —————→	captain finds out, furious he was not told, and retires to his cabin ↓
no resolution, problem recycles	—————— (Becomes) —————→	no resolution, problem recycles until . . . ↓ resolution

Since the isomorphic transformations in our example are concerned only with relationships, and not with context, there are no limitations on the nature of the context or the identity of the characters we use. We could have just as easily selected for the characters in our metaphor a pair of schooners and a sailboat, two trees and a sapling, or a stallion, a mare, and a colt.

Consider another example (an actual case this time) which, because of its straightforewardness, will be used throughout the rest of the book:

> Samuel is a thirty-year-old professional, as is his lover, Kate. Samuel has recently taken on a second professional obligation, which has meant that his work week is now often sixty hours long. Samuel's problem is that, as a result of working longer

hours, he has less time to be with Kate. This has created tension between them which both find very uncomfortable. Now, when they do have time together, most of it is spent bickering. Attempts at discussing the problem also end with both feeling hurt. Samuel wants to keep his job and his lover, wants to make the week twenty hours longer, knows he can't do that, and doesn't know what to do.

In constructing a metaphor for this problem, I chose as a context the "Knights of the Round Table." Notice while examining the set of transformations which follow that had Samuel indicated that Kate was his daughter rather than his lover she could just as easily been assigned the role of "Princess," and that the logical changes in the story line necessitated by her being a princess would naturally follow.

Actual Situation		Metaphor
Samuel ———————	(Becomes) ———→	Lancelot
Kate ———————	(Becomes) ———→	Guenevere
Samuel and Kate ——— are lovers ↓	(Becomes) ———→	Lancelot and Guenevere are lovers ↓
both are ——————— professionals ↓	(Becomes) ———→	Lancelot is a Knight, Guenevere is a Queen ↓
Samuel acquires ——— new responsi- bilities ↓	(Becomes) ———→	King Arthur sends Lancelot off to help with the war in France ↓
sees Kate less ——— ↓	(Becomes) ———→	sees Guenevere less
their relationship ——— becomes strained ↓	(Becomes) ———→	when he does see Guenevere they bicker and are uncomfortable ↓
they try to talk, ——— but end up hurting each other and separating ↓	(Becomes) ———→	Lancelot keeps hoping to correct the situation, but always returns to the Crusades disappointed ↓
no resolution, ——— problem recycles	(Becomes) ———→	no resolution, problem recycles, until . . . . . . ↓ resolution

SECTION 3
The Outcome

All that is missing now to complete the basic metaphor is a *resolution* to the problem. Defining a resolution for a metaphor will depend to some extent upon the purpose for which it is being told (see Part VI). Your personal intuitions regarding useful changes for your client may determine the desired outcome selected. In most cases, however, the client himself will determine the resolution. Usually clients know the changes they want to make. Where they frequently get stuck is in building the bridge between their present, unsatisfactory, recurring situation and the desired situation. All of us have, at one time or another, been so close to the trees that we have missed the forest. One function of a metaphor is to provide a tree-watcher with at least one way to step back and take a look at (and ultimately appreciate) his forest. The resolution, then, has as its two basic components the *desired outcome* and the *strategy* which bridges the gap between the problem and the desired outcome.

When I asked Samuel to tell me how specifically he wanted to change his situation in regards to Kate he explained that he wanted to "feel comfortable and close with her again." So, we now have . . .

Problem	Connecting Strategy	Desired Outcome
Samuel and Kate are bickering about not being together more often	**?**	Samuel wants to keep his jobs and feel comfortable and close to Kate

SECTION 4
The Connecting Strategy

Calibration

In order to get from the client's repetitive problem-situation to the desired outcome, some kind of experiential (behavioral) bridge must be built between the two. It is usually not sufficient to merely jump from "the problem" to "the new behavior." Often this is what the client has been trying (unsuccessfully) to do: "Whenever it starts happening I try to act like it's okay, but I just can't do it." We are here calling the bridge between the problem and the outcome the *connecting strategy*.

One way to understand the connecting strategy is in terms of *calibration* and *recalibration*. Problems are usually recursive. That is, the same or similar configuration of events occurs over and over again, ultimately producing each time the same set of unpleasant or unwanted experiences. This repetitive set of unwanted experiences can be thought of as a cake, and the configuration of events as the ingredients. As ingredients, those events must not only be present in order to produce the cake, they must also be there in the *proper proportions*. Most of the events out of which a problem arises are usually occurring much of the time ("events" being anything from environmental occurrences, to sensations, to perceptions).

For example, a man who "explodes with anger" when "under pressure" is almost certainly under some pressure most of the time (job responsibilities, family responsibilities, personal endeavors, etc.). "Pressure" becomes a problem, however, only when its sources become "too" numerous and/or intense, it is brought to bear on him in "too" preemptory a manner, his ability to cope is "too" preoccupied with other matters, and so on. It is only when these contingencies reach certain proportions in relation to one another that they become "a problem."

The problem, then, is one of "calibration," in that the individual is "set to respond" to a group of events only as they achieve certain proportions. Analogously, only when the air, fuel, and spark reach certain proportions at the proper time will an engine respond by running. Of course, people are not mere engines. But anyone who has had the experience of feeling or acting the "same way" every time they get into "that particular situation" can testify to the fact that those situations seem to *compel* their behavior, rather than merely allow it.

Recalibration

Therefore, in order to alleviate the problem, it must be *recalibrated*. This is the function of the connecting strategy, and it is what allows an individual to get out of a recursive situation so that he can be free to choose. *Recalibrating a recursive situation involves, (1) providing the client with the ability to be aware of when events are proportioning themselves in such a way as to become problematical; and (2) providing the client with a means of reproportioning those events.* In terms of formulating metaphors, the first step in recalibration involves having the character (client) in "some way" break up the old calibration pattern, the result of which is that the character is at last able to effectively change the situation. The "some way" you use will be a product of your experience and intuitions as a people-helper and fellow human being. The second step is to narratively imbue the character with an understanding of the calibration which becomes "a problem" and of the way in which it can be recalibrated.

> . . . Looking back, Mary could see that what had angered her wasn't that her mother asked her to do things (for they were all things she would gladly do), but that her mother wanted them done immediately. Now that Mary knew how to negotiate with her, that would no longer be a problem. . .

The Strategy

Like the outcome, the connecting strategy is also almost always either implied in the client's description of the dynamics of his problem or is inherent in the relationship between the problem and the desired outcome. Looking only at those two factors in Samuel's problem, you can, no doubt, devise several possible strategies which are potentially capable of helping him get what he wants for himself. For instance, Samuel could learn to control his feelings so as not to feel uncomfortable. Or he could give Kate an ultimatum to change her behavior. Or he could even learn to not hear or see Kate when she was angry and hurt. No one of these choices is inherently better than another. The one choice that *is* better than any other, however, is the one that Samuel (or any client) indicates for himself.

When Samuel was asked about how his arguments with Kate usually progressed, he described a typical scene in which he was trying to explain to Kate that this new job of his was very important to him. Kate would then make cracks about Samuel being "such a busy man." After some bickering, they would stop talking altogether and pass a very dull evening. These and other comments made by Samuel indicated that one thing which was probably going on was that Kate was worried that perhaps Samuel's taking on more work meant that he was no longer as fond of her. That was the bridge . . .

Problem	Connecting Strategy	Desired Outcome
Samuel and Kate are bickering about not being together more often	Samuel explicitly tells Kate that he loves and cares about her	Samuel wants to keep his jobs and feel comfortable and close to Kate

As was said above, the desired outcome often presupposes a connecting strategy. But the strategy most likely to succeed will be the one that the client himself directly or indirectly indicates. An excellent way to get that information is to ask the client to describe in detail how he has tried to resolve the problem before. In describing the details of his failure to resolve the problem he will also be implicitly describing what needs to be done in order for the goal to be reached (that is, he will be describing at what points he got stuck and, so, in what ways his model is limited).

Another excellent way to get this information is to ask the client either . . .

What stops you from . . . ("telling her how you feel")?

or . . .

How do you stop yourself from . . . ("feeling relaxed")?

Therapist: What stops you from telling her how you feel?

Client: Well, I guess I'm afraid she'll laugh at me.

In saying, "I'm afraid she'll laugh at me," the client is stating exactly what it is that is standing between his present situation and what he wants for himself. The connecting strategy that this client is indicating for himself, then, is that in some way he overcome or circumvent his fear long enough to do what it is he wants to do (and, presumably, to then find out that there was no need to be afraid in the first place).

SECTION 5
Reframing

A vital component of the metaphor's resolution is *reframing*. To "reframe" is to take a previously painful and unwanted experience or behavior and re-cast it as valuable and potentially useful. What clients often ask for, in terms of changes, is that the therapist somehow help him "get rid of" this or that unpleasant behavior or circumstance. Their requests go something like:

1. If only I didn't get angry, everything would be fine.
2. I don't want to feel sad anymore.
3. I want to feel close to people, but I can't until I can accept them completely.

What each of these clients is asking for in those three sentences is that they be helped to give up some current aspect of their behavior. The first person wants to give up "anger," the second wants to go without "sadness," and the third wishes to relinquish an ability to be "circumspect." This is, however, "throwing the baby out with the bath water." These clients unquestionably have problems with anger, sadness, and circumspection, *but those emotion/behaviors are NOT the problems per se—the problem is in HOW they are using them.* This author chooses as a basic premise for any therapeutic intervention that no emotion, behavior, or experience is inherently "good" or "bad," but that they are all useful when expressed within the appropriate contexts and at the appropriate time. What we are talking about here is the difference between "exchanging one choice for another" and "increasing the client's repertoire of choices."

This is accomplished by explicitly stating to the client (within the context of the metaphor) how the previously unpleasant and/ or inappropriate emotion/behaviors of the past are now useful in terms of the changes which were made. The client who had trouble with "anger," for instance, could be shown that although his original expressions of anger were counterproductive, expressing anger in these "other" situations could be very productive.

> . . . As he looked back over his adventures, he realized that there was now no need for him to vent his anger in that situation anymore. He also gained strength and self-assurance from the knowledge that if he *did* want or need to be angry, in that or any situation, that he had within him the power and resourcefulness to do it. Now *he* could call the shots . . . .

By using a few lines such as these, what was once considered a liability becomes an asset. For you, as a therapist assisting others to change, learning to effectively reframe experiences means learning to appreciate the potential usefulness of any emotion, behavior, or experience.

So, the entire process of formulating a basic metaphor is:

A. Gather Information
1. Identify the significant persons involved
    a. identify their inter-personal relationships.
2. Identify the events that are characteristic of the problem situation
    a. specify how the problem progresses (calibration)
3. Specify what changes the client wants to make (the outcome)
    a. make sure that they are well-formed

    4. Identify what the client has done in the past to cope with the problem, OR what "stops" the client from making the desired changes (may indicate connecting strategy)

B. Build the Metaphor

    1. Select a context

    2. Populate and plot the metaphor so that it is isomorphic with A_1, A_2, and A_3 above

    3. Determine a resolution, including . . .

        a. a strategy for recalibration (from A_4 above)

        b. the desired outcome (from A_3 above)

        c. and reframing of the original problem situation

C. Tell It

    1. Using the syntactic patterns of . . .

        a. lack of referential index

        b. unspecified verbs

        c. nominalizations

        d. imbedded commands and marking

        . . . all of which are described in the next section . . .

SECTION 6
The Syntax of Metaphors[2]

Using The Transderivational Search

What makes it possible for a metaphor to be influential is that it is isomorphic with the client's actual situation. We have spent most of Part II learning how to make a direct crossover from the characteristics of the client's problem to those of the metaphor in an effort to insure that similarity. However, recall from Part I the point made regarding one person's inability to know what exactly is going on in another person's head. The isomorphism that the therapist has so carefully built into the metaphor covers the sequence of events but it is *not* reliable in terms of providing an accurate rendering of how the client *experiences those events*. In Samuel's case, for instance, it is relatively simple to provide a metaphor in which the flow of action is very nearly the same as that in the actual situation. But when it comes to specifically describing that action we have little or no information as to what description will best coincide with the ways in which Samuel experiences them. The approach that gets us out from under this limitation is to *not be specific* (in the following specific ways).

As was said in Part I, human beings both consciously and unconsciously constantly try to make sense out of their sensory and perceptual experience. In so doing, people use the only yardstick they have at their disposal for measuring and evaluating the significance of their experiences—that yardstick is their personal *model of the world*. The process of *using* that yardstick is what we have already described as the *transderivational search*. By intentionally refraining from specifying particular information, actions, and experiences of the characters within the metaphor, we force its audience to derive and employ their own interpretations of what is "really going on." (Similarly, my not explaining the nature of Peugeot doors to my friend in Part I forced him to make the best sense he could of his experience.) Since the metaphor is for the client, only his rendering of it can be exactly correct. As the tailor, your job is to select the material and to properly cut-out the pattern for the garment. In this case, however, it is the customer who does the alterations so that the garment fits.

Lack of Referential Index

Words which have a "referential index" are nouns or phrases which specifically name something in the client's experience. Consider the following two sentences:

1) Someone was lurking in a room of the house.
2) His siamese-twin brother, John, was lurking in the closet.

There is little information in sentence (1) which can be used to determine "who" is involved and "where"—that is, both the "someone" and the "room" do not refer to anyone or anything specific. On the other hand, sentence (2) leaves little doubt as to "who" and "where." The second sentence supplies the referential indices that are missing in the first sentence. Although such specification of experience is invaluable when gathering information about a client's situation, it can be disruptive when telling a metaphor. For example, suppose that in your narrative a character is hiding in a house *and* that it is not significant where he is hiding. If you then describe him as "hiding in the broom closet" while your client was thinking "hiding-under-the-bed" a mismatch between your narrative and the client's experience of it has been created. This can be easily avoided by making the noun "room" non-referring. For instance, "Then he ran into the house and hid *somewhere*." Now the client is free to put "him" wherever "he belongs" in the house, and you and he are in complete agreement.

As already indicated above, it is not intended that you reduce all the nouns in your narrative to "person," "place," and "thing." The point is that when the specification of a noun is insignificant to the course of the story, there is no benefit in going to the trouble to do so. In fact, because of the transderivational phenomenon, you will almost certainly increase the meaningfulness of the story by leaving those nouns to the vagaries of the client's imagination.

Unspecified Verbs

Just as words lacking a referential index are specified by asking of them "who?," "what?," and "where?," verbs which are *unspecified* are specified by asking "how?" or "in what way?" Verbs describe *how* something is acting or existing in the world. As in the case of nouns, verbs can be more or less specified depending upon the purpose of the description:

1) John went into the closet.

2) John crept up to the closet, gently opened the door, then jumped in, head first, using his feet to slam the door behind him.

Here again the second sentence leaves little doubt as to how John got himself into the closet. Although it is a bizarre and entertaining description it may not coincide with how the client would get John into that closet. Provided that *how* John gets closeted is insignificant to the story, the first sentence is preferable since it allows the client the freedom to choose the manner of John's entrance.

Nominalizations

When describing a personal experience we often take "process" words and talk about them as though they were "things" or "events." Thus, "I feel" becomes "a *feeling*," "I am hoping" becomes "I have a *hope*," and "I was angry" becomes "I had *anger*." Although we can talk about feelings, hope, and anger as though they are things that we can hold in our hands, they are actually processes which are dynamic and intangible. One cannot take an anger, or an awareness, or a pain, and put it out on a table for all to walk around and inspect. To do that to a process word is to *nominalize* it.

Although nominalizing one's experience is often not very helpful, it can be helpful in metaphors for the following reason: Nominalizations initiate transderivational searches since inherent in a nominalization are deletions of important information needed to make sense out of the word. In the statement, "I had anger," for instance, what is deleted and must be filled in are "angry at whom?," "angry about what?," "angry when?," and "angry in what way?" Consider this pair of sentences:

1) With his jump into the closet came an awareness of his situation.

2) As he jumped into the closet, John became gradually aware that he did not know if he was going after, or getting away from, something.

In the first sentence, the process of "being aware" is turned into the event or thing, "awareness." By nominalizing "aware" we leave out information as to *who* is being aware of *what specifically* and in *what way*? This information is included in the second sentence, which describes a process John is going through. As in the other language distinctions we have already mentioned, using nominalizations in metaphors gives the client the opportunity to turn the nominalized word into a process of his own choosing.

Imbedded Commands and Marking

Since metaphors are essentially a vehicle for indirectly suggesting and/or implementing changes in patterns of coping there are usually several places in the narrative (particularly in the resolution) where an important idea is being stressed. One way to draw the client's attention to that suggestion, and to increase its power, is to make it part of an *imbedded command*. Imbedded commands are formed by inserting the client's name (or, in some cases, "you") into the sentence in such a way as to make all that follows in the sentence a directive to the client. For example:

1) After sitting in there awhile, he decided to come out.

2) After sitting in there awhile, he decided to, <u>David, come out</u>. (Underlining indicates change in voice tonality. Read aloud for proper effect.)

By pausing long enough in the middle of sentence (2) to insert "David" we make what follows a direct statement to the client: "David, come out."

Similar to imbedded commands is the concept of *marking*. "Marking" refers to emphasizing specific words or phrases by coinciding changes in the therapist's tonality (or by making specific sounds, gestures, or contacts with the client) with those parts of the message to be given special attention. In a metaphor there are usually incidents, concepts, or characters which are especially important in terms of the client relating his own experiences to those in the story. These incidents can be marked to draw them to the conscious or unconscious attention of the client (read the examples aloud):

1) And when he came out this time, he came all the way out.

2) And when he came out this time, he came <u>ALL THE WAY OUT.</u>

SECTION 7
Samuel's Metaphor

Now that we have (A) gathered the necessary information regarding Samuel's problem, and have (B) built our metaphor for him, all that is left to do is (C) tell it.

In order to assist you in becoming familiar with the patterns of syntax described in the previous section, they are noted beside each sentence in which they occur in the following tale. (Note that being aware of these patterns cuts both ways since they can be used both in assisting the client in specifying his problem situation and in initiating transderivational search.) It is suggested that you first read the story without considering the syntactic patterns, attending only to its structural aspects (i.e., isomorphism, connecting strategy, outcome, and reframing). Then, reread the story and look specifically for syntactic patterns in each sentence. Covering up the column of answers until you have made your own determination of the patterns will help you to become adept at recognizing and using them.

L = lack of referential index
U = unspecified verb
N = nominalization

In England, in the time of King Arthur's	N-time
famous Round Table, there was a Knight of	
honor and greatness known as Sir Lancelot.	N-honor, greatness
No doubt you've heard of him. Lancelot's	N-doubt; L-him
lover was Queen Guenevere. Lancelot and	N-lover
Guenevere had shared many hardships and	U-shared; N-hardships
triumphs, were the closest of friends, and	N-triumphs, U-closest
loved one another very much.	
One being a Knight and the other	L-one, other
being royalty, both naturally had many duties	U-being; L-both; N-duties
and functions for which they were responsible.	N-functions; L-they; U-responsible
They saw to it that the things which needed	L-they, things; U-saw to it
to be done were properly taken care of.	U-properly taken care of
Each in their own way, they	L-each, their, way, they
took care of the people and, in	U-took care; L-people
many ways, were taken care of by the	L-ways; U-taken care of
people. Lancelot took great pride in	L-people; N-pride
this responsibility of his, and was	N-responsibility; L-this, his
rewarded for his efforts with the	U-rewarded; N-efforts L-his
respect, affection, and support of the	N-respect, affection, support
people.	L-people
These duties did occupy much of	N-duties; U-occupy; L-these
Lancelot's time, but whenever he could,	L-whenever, he
he would spend time with Guenevere.	U-spend time; L-he
These times were very special to both	L-these times; U-special
of them, since both realized that such	L-them, both
close and loving ties between two people	U-close; N-ties; L-two people
are not easily found.	
Now it came to pass that Lancelot was	U-came to pass; L-it
called upon by King Arthur to fight in France.	U-called upon, fight

He went, and was happy to do so, for he — L-he

recognized that he had responsibilities — N-responsibilities; L-he
L-responsibilities

to the Kingdom and to himself that in

many ways superceded those of his — L-many ways, those, his,

other duties. His greatest regret was — L-other duties; N-regret;
L-his

that now he would be seeing less of — L-he; U-seeing less

Guenevere.

As often as he could, Lancelot would — L-often, he

return home to see Guenevere. But

Guenevere had become bitter over being left — U-left

behind and alone. Instead of the joy and — U-behind, alone; N-joy

pleasure of past times, their reunions — N-pleasure, past times,
reunions; L-their

were marked by arguments and tension. — N-arguments, tension
U-marked

Both became uncomfortable. He — U-uncomfortable; L-both,
L-he

continued to return to Guenevere whenever — L-whenever

he could, but each time he did, Lancelot's — L-he

eager anticipation of his visit waned a — N-anticipation, visit; L-his

little more. Lancelot knew that if they — L-they

continued the way they had been, he and — L-way, they, he

Guenevere would soon be asunder. — U-asunder

One day Lancelot became weary of — L-one day

battling in France and set off for

another visit home. He was disheartened — N-visit; U-disheartened
L-he, home

and tired, and he hoped that he could — U-tired; L-he

find relaxation in the company of — N-relaxation, company

Guenevere. When they were together — L-they

again, however, it became the same old — L-it; U-became

uncomfortable situation. At last Lancelot — N-situation; L-at last

could stand it no longer. He made Guenevere — L-it, he; U-made...sit down

sit down and then told her, Samuel, "Now I — L-her

want you to listen to me for a moment. I'm — L-you

not at all happy about being separated from — U-separated

you as much as I am, but I also know — L-you, as much as; U-know

that what I am doing is important. I've	L-what I am doing
wracked my brains trying to come up with	
a way to solve this problem and I'm not	L-this; N-problem
at all sure what to do. The only thing	
I know to do is to tell you that you are	L-you
very important to me, that I love you,	U-important; L-me, you
and that just because I am away doesn't	L-away
mean that I don't care about you, because	U-care; L-you
I do. Here or gone, I think of you often.	L-here, gone, you, often
And if I could always have you near me,	U-think
I would."	
Upon hearing this Guenevere's eyes	L-this
filled with tears and she embraced	L-she
him. "All this time," she said, Samuel,	L-him, this time, she
"I thought that you never gave me a	L-you, me
thought when you were gone . . . That	N-thought; L-you, gone
perhaps you were glad to be rid of	L-you
me for awhile."	L-me, awhile
Of course, from then on their love	L-then on, their; N-love
and friendship grew. In fact, they were	N-friendship; U-grew;
	L-they
closer than ever before, since both,	U-closer; L-ever before,
	both
Samuel, had learned that there was never	
any reason for one to refrain from telling	L-one; U-refrain; N-reason
the other exactly what was bothering	L-other, what
her or what he felt. And even though	L-her, what, he
they weren't together as much as had	L-they, as much;
	U-together
once been the case now when they did	L-once, they
get together they took advantage of their	U-get together, took advan-
	tage; L-they, their
time to enjoy one another more than	N-time; U-enjoy
ever before.	

This metaphor is an adequate isomorphic representation of Samuel's problem. It also includes a means of resolving the problem. The story as it now stands may or may not prove to be an adequate learning experience for Samuel, depending upon Samuel's ability to utilize the information, the presence of unaccounted-for significant contingencies in the problem situation, and the therapist's purpose in telling the metaphor. One way to enhance the effectiveness of the story is to include in its framework the dimensions of "Satir categories," "representational systems," and "submodalities." The importance, in terms of significance, resolution, and thoroughness, of metaphors operating at several levels was discussed in Part I. So that you can better discern the contribution of each of the levels to be added, we will add each in turn to Samuel's metaphor at the ends of the next three parts.

FOOTNOTES TO PART II

1. It is strongly recommended that you refer to *The Structure of Magic, Vol. 1*, by Bandler and Grinder, chapters 2, 3, and 4. These chapters present an explicit model for gathering the maximum amount of useful information from your clients. This skill is an essential starting point regardless of the therapeutic approach you use as all interventions you make are either consciously or unconsciously based on what you have learned about your client and his problem situation.

2. A more complete description and discussion of trans-derivational phenomena and of the communication patterns introduced in this section can be found in *The Structure of Magic, Vol. I* and in *Patterns of the Hypnotic Techniques of Milton H. Erickson, M.D., Vol. I*, both by Richard Bandler and John Grinder, and in *Patterns, Vol. II*, by Grinder, DeLozier, and Bandler.

PART III
ADDING SATIR CATEGORIES

PROLOGUE

By Mother Goose

The Queen of Hearts
She made some tarts,
All on a summer's day;
The Knave of Hearts
He stole the tarts,
And took them clean away
The King of Hearts
Called for the Tarts,
And beat the Knave full sore;
The Knave of Hearts
Brought back the tarts,
And vow'd he'd steal no more.
The King of Spades
He kissed the maids,
Which made the Queen full sore;
The Queen of Spades
She beat those maids,
And turned them out of door.
The Knave of Spades
Grieved for those jades,
And did for them implore;
The Queen so gent
She did relent
And vow'd she'd ne'er strike more.
The King of Clubs
He often drubs
His loving Queen and wife;

The Queen of Clubs
Returns his snubs,
And all is noise and strife;
The Knave of Clubs
Gives winks and rubs,
And swears he'll take her part;
For when our Kings
Will do such things,
They should be made to smart.
The Diamond King
I fain would sing,
And likewise his fair Queen;
But that the Knave,
a haughty slave,
Must needs step in between;
Good Diamond King
With hempen string
The haughty Knave destroy!
Then may your Queen
With mind serene,
Your royal bed enjoy.

ADDING SATIR CATEGORIES

When one person communicates with another that communication has two components—its *content* and its *style*. The content of the communication is whatever information the individual is contributing to the topic of conversation. The *style* is the *way* in which that content is communicated. Communication style, as it is being used here, includes voice tonality, body gestures and posture, facial expression, and characteristic patterns of syntax. As you probably know from personal experience, the style of a communication can have tremendous effect on the listener's interpretation of its content. Notice how these factors affect the following simple request:

1) "Get me that jar?"   (speaker looks wide-eyed, has palms upturned and choked voice)

2) "Get me that jar!"   (Speaker is glowering, talking very loud, and is pointing at jar)

3) "Get me that jar."   (speaker's face is impassive, voice monotone, and jerks thumb over shoulder without looking up)

Every communication, then, is accompanied by stylistic components which affect, and are often part of, its message. That much is obvious. What may not be as apparent is that *people consistently use styles of communication which are different for, and characteristic of, each individual.* Take a moment to recall recent conversations with acquaintances, but pay attention only to the *ways* in which they expressed themselves (that is, their style). You will probably notice that some or all of their styles are dif-

65

ferent, and that all were consistent in their use of their particular style.

Although we are all different in the ways in which we communicate there are also some styles that are sufficiently consistent and so generally characteristic of human communication that they can be formalized as patterns or "modes" of communication. People vary in the ways in which they communicate *and* there are some consistencies in those variations. By formalizing those consistencies into patterns they become available to us as yardsticks with which styles of communication can be measured. This formalization of styles into communication modes has been done for us by Virginia Satir. I could do no better here than to quote her own excellent explanation of these patterns.

SECTION 1
The Satir Categories

(1) PLACATER

Words Agree
     ("Whatever you
     want is okay. I
     am just here to
     make you happy.")

Body Placates
     ("I am helpless.")

Insides ("I feel like a noth-
     ing; without him I
     am dead. I am worth-
     less.")

The *placater* always talks in an ingratiating way, trying to please, apologizing, never disagreeing, no matter what. He's a "yes man." He talks as though he could do nothing for himself; he must always get someone to approve of him. You will find later that if you play this role for even five minutes, you will begin to feel nauseous and want to vomit.

A big help in doing a good placating job is to think of yourself as really worth nothing. You are lucky just to be allowed to eat. You owe everybody gratitude, and you really are responsible for everything that goes wrong. You know you could have stopped the rain if you used your brains, but you don't have any. Naturally you will agree with any criticism made about you. You are, of course, grateful for the fact that anyone even talks to you, no matter what they say or how they say it. You would not think of asking anything for yourself. After all, who are you to ask? Besides, if you can just be good enough it will come by itself.

Be the most syrupy, martyrish, bootlicking person you can be. Think of yourself as being physically down on one knee, wobbling a bit, putting out one hand in a begging fashion, and be sure to have your head up so your neck will hurt and your eyes will become strained so in no time at all you will begin to get a headache.

When you talk in this position your voice will be whiny and squeaky because you keep your body in such a lowered position that you don't have enough air to keep a rich, full voice. You will be saying "yes" to everything, no matter what you feel or think. The placating stance is the body position that matches the placating response.

(2) BLAMER

Words   Disagree
("You never do
anything right. What
is the matter with
you?")

Body   Blames
("I am the boss
around here.")

Insides   ("I am lonely and
unsuccessful")

The *blamer* is a fault-finder, a dictator, a boss. He acts superior, and he seems to be saying, "If it weren't for you, everything would be all right." The internal feeling is one of tightness in the muscles and in the organs. Meanwhile the blood pressure is increasing. The voice is hard, tight, and often shrill and loud.

Good blaming requires you to be as loud and tyrannical as you can. Cut everything and everyone down.

As a blamer it would be helpful to think of yourself pointing your finger accusingly and to start your sentences with "You never do this or you always do that or why do you always or why do you never . . . " and so on. Don't bother about an answer. That is unimportant. The blamer is much more interested in throwing his weight around than really finding out about anything.

Whether you know it or not, when you are blaming you are breathing in little tight spurts, or holding your breath altogether, because your throat muscles are so tight. Have you ever seen a really first-rate blamer whose eyes were bulging, neck muscles and nostrils standing out, who was getting red and whose voice sounded like someone shoveling coal? Think of yourself standing with one hand on your hip and the other arm extended with your index finger pointed straight out. Your face is screwed up, your lips curled, your nostrils flared as you tell, call names, and criticize everything under the sun . . . You don't really feel you are worth anything, either. So if you can get someone to obey you, then you feel you count for something.

(3) COMPUTER

Words   Ultra reasonable ("If one were to observe carefully, one might notice the workworn hands of someone present here.")

Body   computes ("I'm calm, cool, and collected.")

Insides   ("I feel vulnerable.")

The *computer* is very correct, very reasonable with no semblance of any feeling showing. He is calm, cool, and collected. He could be compared to an actual computer or a dictionary. The body feels dry, often cool, and disassociated. The voice is a dry monotone, and the words are likely to be abstract.

When you are a computer, use the longest words possible, even if you aren't sure of their meanings. You will at least sound intelligent. After one paragraph no one will be listening anyway. To get yourself really in the mood for this role, imagine that your spine is a long, heavy steel rod reaching from your buttocks to the nape of your neck, and you have a ten-inch-wide iron collar around your neck. Keep everything about yourself as motionless as possible, including your mouth. You will have to try hard to keep your hands from moving, but do it.

When you are computing, your voice will naturally go dead because you have no feeling from the cranium down. Your mind is bent on being careful not to move, and you are kept busy choosing the right word. After all, you should never make a mistake. The sad part of this role is that it seems to represent an ideal goal for many people. "Say the right words; show no feeling; don't react."

(4) DISTRACTER

Words	Irrelevant (the words make no sense)
Body	Angular and off somewhere else
Insides	("Nobody cares. There is no place for me.")

Whatever the *distracter* does or says is irrelevant to what anyone else is saying or doing. He never makes a response to the point. His internal feeling is one of dizziness. The voice can be singsong, often out of tune with the words, and can go up and down without reason because it is focused nowhere.

When you play the distracting role, it will help you to think of yourself as a kind of lopsided top, constantly spinning, but never knowing where you are going, and not realizing it when you get there. You are too busy moving your mouth, your body, your arms, your legs. Make sure you are never on the point with your words. Ignore everyone's questions; maybe come back with one of your own on a different subject. Take a piece of imaginary lint off someone's garment, untie shoelaces, and so on.

Think of your body as going off in different directions at once. Put your knees together in an exaggerated knock-kneed fashion. This will bring your buttocks out, and make it easy for you to hunch your shoulders and have your arms and hands going in opposite directions.

At first this role seems like a relief, but after a few minutes of play, the terrible loneliness and purposelessness arise. If you can keep yourself moving fast enough, you won't notice it so much.

As practice for yourself, take the four physical stances I have described, hold them for just sixty seconds and see what happens to you. Since many people are unaccustomed to feeling their body reactions, you may find at first that you are so busy thinking you aren't feeling. Keep at it, and you will begin to have the internal feelings you've experienced so many times before. Then the moment you are on your own two feet and are freely relaxed and able to move, you find your internal feeling changes.

It is my hunch that these ways of communicating are learned early in childhood. As the child tries to make his way through the complicated and often threatening world in which he finds himself, he uses one or another of these means of communicating. After enough use he can no longer distinguish his response from his feeling of worth or his personality.

Use of any of these four responses forges another ring in an individual's feeling of low self-worth or low pot.

Attitudes prevalent in our society also reinforce these ways of communicating—many of which are learned at our mother's knee.

"Don't impose; it's selfish to ask for things for yourself," helps to reinforce placating.

"Don't let anyone put you down; don't be a coward," helps to reinforce blaming.

"Don't be serious. Live it up! Who cares?" helps to reinforce distracting.

At this point you may well be wondering if there is any hope for us at all if these four crippling modes of communication are all we have. Of course they are not.

There is a fifth response that I have called *leveling* or flowing. In this response all parts of the message are going in the same direction—the voice says words that match the facial expression, the body position, and the voice tone. Relationships are easy, free and honest, and there are few threats to self-esteem. With this response there is no need to blame, retreat into a computer, or to be in perpetual motion.

Of the five responses only the leveling one has any chance to heal ruptures, break impasses, or build bridges between people. And lest leveling seem too unrealistic to you, let me assure you that you can still placate if you choose, blame if you like, be on a head trip, or be distracting. The difference is you know what you are doing and are prepared to take the consequences for it.

[from *Peoplemaking*, pp. 63-73; Science and Behavior Books]

SECTION 2
Satir Categories and Therapy

Usually when a person comes in requesting help in changing the changes he wants to make take the general form of . . .

I experience *this* now.

I want to make an exchange and instead experience *that* from now on.

One way to talk about these two statements of experience is to say that they represent two different *parts* of the person who made them. For example, if we filled in the *this* and *that* with some pair of specific experiences we would get statements similar to the following:

I experience *depression* now.

I want to make an exchange and instead experience *happiness* from now on.

Or, more prosaically:

"I should be happy, but I can't be because I feel depressed so much."

Part of what this person is saying is that there is a part of him that "feels depressed," *and* a part that wants to "be happy." To call them "parts" of a person is of course arbitrary—a way of talking about the distinctions we are making between two or more different experiences. When distinguishing one experience from another we could just as simply and accurately call them "personality aspects," "characteristics," "ego involvements," or "organs." The point is that in understanding another person's experience it is useful to be able to recognize what constitutes for that person one experience and what constitutes another experience.

Our understanding of "parts" allows us to make excellent use of Satir categories in formulating effective therapeutic metaphors.[1] In the author's experience most or all of the parts belonging to a person will have associated with it one of the Satir categories. Just as individuals have characteristic ways of expressing themselves, so does an individual express different aspects of his or her experience (that is, their "parts") in ways which are characteristic. In order to understand this better it is first necessary to know more about how it is possible to tell that one or another Satir category is being used to express a part.

There are many ways to determine what Satir category any particular part is operating out of. Digital[2] cues include direct statements which specify that part's Satir mode (such as, "I only consider cerebral matters"—computing, or, "I prostrate myself before you"—placating), and the use of certain cue words which imply particular Satir stances. Some of these cue words with examples for each category are:

Placater: qualifiers; IF, ONLY, JUST, EVEN, etc. subjunctive verbs; COULD, WOULD, etc.

"If only she would be happy then I could be happy."

"Would you like me to do that for you?"

Blamer: universal qualifiers; ALL, EVERY, ANY, EACH TIME, etc.

negative questions; HOW COME YOU CAN'T . . . ? WHY DON'T YOU . . .?, etc. imperatives; SHOULD, MUST, etc.

"I should be happy."

"Every time you do that you look foolish. Why don't you stop?"

Computer: leaves out self as the experiencer or object of experience:

I understand → AS CAN BE UNDERSTOOD or, *confuses me* → IS CONFUSING.

non-referring nouns; IT, HE, SHE, ONE. nominalizations of experiences:

tense → TENSION; *quick* → QUICKNESS; *hoping* → HAVE HOPE; etc.

"It is quite clear to anyone that this is a problem of depression."

"What does one do when one has no more hope?"

Distractor: Frequently a rapid alternation of the above three categories. Also, neglects to refer to the content of the therapist's question or statement.

> T: And how do you feel about her leaving you?
>
> C: "Did you know I've got a new car?"

Analogue[3] cues are also important indicators of the Satir category being expressed. These cues include physical gestures such as a pointing finger (blaming), a palm-up hand (placating), an unmoving body (computing), and a constantly moving body (distracting). Analogue cues also include speaking tonalities. Obvious examples of these are yelling (blaming), a very soft voice (placating), a monotonous and deliberate speaking voice (computing), and sing-song chatter (distracting). These are only a few examples of analogical correlates of Satir stances. As you begin to use these distinctions you will be able to make subtle discriminations of analogue cues.

(One very direct way of determining the Satir category associated with a particular part experience is to simply ask, "What are you aware of feeling as you say that?" The response to this question usually provides the necessary information; e.g., "helpless," "angry," "nothing," and "what?")

There are two ways in which knowing the Satir category through which a person or a part expresses itself can be useful in effective metaphor building. First, it allows you to make the story more significant for the client. By making these modes of communication characteristic of the story's protagonists you will be making it more understandable and acceptable to the client as an accurate representation of his situation. This is because the characters in the metaphor are communicating in ways which are similar to the ways in which the people and parts which are relevant to the client's situation are communicating. Let's use Joe again as an example. Suppose Joe said:

> Joe: If she would just look happier, then every time I get home I wouldn't get so angry . . . I shouldn't get so angry. (as he finishes, Joe points at himself and raises his voice.)

In this sentence Joe shows us a placating part which *would* like his wife to be happier, and a blaming part which condemns him for getting *so* angry.[4] Now if we were going to tell him a metaphorical fairytale about a prince and a princess, Joe would probably make more personal sense out of it if the prince spoke lovingly and hopefully about the princess until each time he joined her after being away—at which time the prince lost control and besmirched her. A story in which the prince besmirched his princess *until* they were reunited would have much less relevance for Joe, no matter how entertaining it may be. And the story's resolution will consequently also be of less significance. So, maintaining Satir category parallels between the actual problem and the tale helps insure the relevance of the metaphor.

The second way in which Satir categories can be helpful is in utilizing metaphors to assist in the process of change. Often individuals "have a problem" coping within a particular situation, not because of a lack of choices about *what* to do but because of a lack of choices about *how* to do it. The problem, then, is not the content of what the person is saying or doing, but (at least in part) the way (style) in which that content is being communicated. For instance, a person who wants to be able to feel comfortable talking with people he considers to be intellectual or professional superiors will probably be at a disadvantage if he incorporates a placating (or blaming, or distracting) stance into his communications with them. In most cases a computing mode of communication would be the most appropriate since that is the level at which most of "their" conversations operate. Similarly, the individual who blames when stopped by a policeman is more likely to be cited than one who knows how to effectively placate (or even compute or distract). So if, as you aid a client in specifying his problem, you determine that he is using a mode of communication which is inappropriate for the experience being sought, you can make as part of your strategy for assisting them *a switch in Satir category to one more likely to be effective.*

Following is a list of sentences which you can use to begin to attune yourself to identifying Satir categories. It is suggested that you cover up the right hand column (which identifies the Satir category and key words for each sentence) until you have made your own determination of the communication mode being represented. As you do so, notice that in some sentences there are indications of the Satir stance of another person besides the speaker, or of two or more parts of the speaker.

1) It's not surprising that one would feel guilt about sex, if one were confronted with such a man right off the bat.

computing:
    one; guilt;
    such a man

2) Most people you see these days don't get as scattered as you always do.

blaming:
    as you always do

3) I would notice a little bit of a nice self-image if I could.

placating
    would; could

4) I hear what you're saying, but it doesn't sound right!
(speaker at first upturns palms, then ends by pointing and raising voice)

first part, placates:
    upturned palms
second part, blames:
    pointing and loud voice

5) A lovely looking woman does, of course, please the eye.

computing:
    the eye

6) Every time I try to talk some sense into her, Joan just keeps bringing up absurd comments about this and that.

speaker, blames:
    every time
Joan, distracts:
    'just brings up this and that'

7) Why don't they knock that eyesore of a building down?

blaming:
    why don't they

8) Sometimes I would try and try to focus my attention on what they had to say. You know, every time I did that, though, I became very sharp with them and cut them down!
(speaker points at therapist during last sentence)

first part, placates:
    would

second part, blames:
    every time; *points at therapist*

9) If only my stereo produced as crisp a sound as those do.
(speaker's voice is whiny)

placating:
    if only;
    whining

10) Well *I* did everything to get us all back into the picture, damnit! But that's over now. Since some individuals have shown an unwillingness to cooperate, there is no need for such efforts to continue. *(glowers and talks loudly in first sentence, then folds his arms across his chest and talks evenly)*

first part, blames: *glowers, talks loudly*

second part, computes: some; unwillingness; efforts; *folded arms*

SECTION 3
Satir Categories in Metaphor

The importance of Satir categories in building metaphors is that they describe a model which is capable of *characterizing* our individual patterns of communication. In addition to typical, or characteristic, modes of communication, people evidence *situationally dependent* communication stances as well. Everyone at some time and in some particular context has placated, blamed, computed, and distracted. These modes of communication are a part of the description of the significant persons and experiences cast in the client's problem. As partial descriptions of personal ways of communication, Satir category distinctions in metaphors can be helpful to the client in distinguishing one character from another, and in its enhancement of the isomorphism of the story.

Satir categories are not only enhancing but *can be used to effect changes on a level besides that of the basic story.* What frequently interferes with an individual's ability to make personal changes and/or to effectively communicate with others (or himself) is *not* the content of what is being said or not said, but rather the *way* in which it is being communicated. The strategy for incorporating Satir stance changes into a metaphor is to (1) characterize each of the story's protagonists in terms of the communication modes used by their counterparts in the "real" situation, then (2) *make whatever changes occur in the resolution contingent upon appropriate changes in Satir category.*

Let us take Samuel's problem as a clarifying example. It was quite clear from his gestures, tonality, and syntax that he communicates as a placater in his relationship with Kate. On the other hand, Samuel's description of Kate's gestures, tonality and syntax indicated that she frequently blames when he communicates with her. These are the same communication patterns that they have been using (unsuccessfully) to try to resolve their problem. The fairytale, then, becomes an opportunity for Samuel to metaphorically experience a different mode of communication. What that different mode will be depends upon the nature of the problem and the desired outcome. The information from Samuel, for instance, indicates that he and Kate need to "level" with one another about what they are thinking and feeling, and that Samuel will have to temporarily switch into another communication stance ("blaming") in order for that to become possible (that is, in order to get Kate to listen). The strategy, then, is . . .

METAPHOR	Connecting Strategy	RESOLUTION Outcome
Samuel — Placating	Blaming	Leveling
Kate — Blaming	Placating	Leveling

By using this strategy Samuel has the opportunity to increase his repertoire of communication skills (in the context of dealing with Kate) to include "blaming" and "leveling."

Incorporating Satir categories into a metaphor is easily done. Once you have specified for yourself the Satir stances of significant persons or parts in the problem and have specified your strategy for modal changes, simply indicate in your descriptions of the cast, or in your descriptions of their actions, the patterns which typify their modes of communication. Thus, "John said" becomes "John *whined*," or "John *yelled*," or "John *reasoned*," or "John *babbled*."

Let us now return to Samuel's story and include in it this new dimension. As in Part II, alongside of the tale are key words which indicate what Satir category is being represented.

SECTION 4
The Return of Samuel's Metaphor

Satir Category
P — placating
B — blaming
L — leveling

In England, in the time of King Arthur's famous
Round Table, there was a Knight of honor and
greatness known as Sir Lancelot. No doubt
you've heard of him. Lancelot's lover was
Queen Guenevere. Lancelot and Guenevere had
shared many hardships and triumphs, were the
closest of friends, and loved one another very
much.

In many ways they were alike, and in others
they were quite different. Both enjoyed many
of the same pastimes, and the same kinds of
foods, and both loved to converse. Lancelot
would usually hang back somewhat during   P-would hang back
these talks. Of course, on the field he was
invincible. But it was somehow different
with Guenevere. It was not that he had less
to say — it was just that Guenevere could be   P-just, could
so overpowering and stubborn. Lancelot   B-overpowering, stubborn;
would say to himself, "I'm sure she would be   P-would,would
glad to hear my views if it was important   P-if important
to do so."

One being a Knight and the other being
royalty, both naturally had many duties and
functions for which they were responsible.
They saw to it that the things which needed
to be done were properly taken care of. Each
in their own way, they took care of the people
and, in many ways, were taken care of by the
people. Lancelot took great pride in this responsibility of his, and was rewarded for his efforts
with the respect, affection, and support of the
people.

These duties did occupy much of Lancelot's
time but, whenever he could, he would spend　　　P-could, would
time with Guenevere. During his frequent
visits to the castle it was usually Guenevere who
decided for them how they would occupy them-　　B-decided for them
selves, which was fine with Lancelot, for he was
happy just to be with his friend and lover. These　　P-just
times were very special to both of them, since
both realized that such close and loving ties
between two people are not easily found.

Now one day it came to pass that Lancelot
was called into the presence of King Arthur.
The King looked at Lancelot with tired eyes
and said, "Once again England requires your
service. You know that we are now engaged
in conflict with France, and it is to those shores
that England . . . and I . . . now ask you to
travel, there to take command of the field."

Lancelot went, and was glad to do so, for he
recognized that he had responsibilities to the
Kingdom and to himself that in many ways
superceded those of his other duties. His greatest regret was that now he would be seeing less
of Guenevere.

As often as he could Lancelot would return　　P-could, would
home to see Guenevere. But she had become
bitter over being left behind and alone. Instead
of the joy and pleasure of past times, their reunions were marked by arguments and tension.
As the situation deteriorated, Lancelot began
trying everything he could think of just to　　　P-could, just to please
please her. But Guenevere seemed to become
even more angry when he tried to appease and　　B-angry; P-appease
please her than when he didn't. Guenevere's　　　P-please
usual comment went something like, "Why　　　　B-why don't you
don't you stop mewing about, eh? Any time　　　　B-any
you get bored you should just go on back to　　　　B-you should
France." Both became very uncomfortable.

Of course, Lancelot did go back to France.
He continued to return to see Guenevere whenever he could, but each time he did, his eager　　　P-could

anticipation of his visit waned a little more.
Lancelot knew that if they continued the way
they had been, he and Guenevere would soon
be asunder.

One day Lancelot became weary of battling
in France and set off for another visit home. He
was disheartened and tired, and he hoped that
he could find relaxation in the company of   P-could
Guenevere. When they were together again it
became the same old uncomfortable situation.
At last Lancelot could stand it no longer. He
suddenly, Samuel, stood up, shook his finger   B-shook his finger
at Guenevere and bellowed, "That's it! This   B-bellowed
has got to stop now! This time, by Merlin, *you*   B-you will
will be quiet and listen to me. Every time this   B-every
has happened in the past, you have done all
the ranting and raving. And now it's my turn!
You sit there a moment and open your ears to   B-you sit
what I have to tell you." Guenevere shrank   P-shrank
back at this unexpected explosion of Lancelot's,   B-explosion
and sat meekly while he had his say.   P-meekly

Lancelot continued to pace and gesture as
he exclaimed, "I'm not at all happy about being   B-exclaimed
separated from you as much as I am, but I also
know that what I am doing is important. And
as a result we have been in a mess." Lancelot put
his hands to his head and continued, "I've wracked my brains trying to come up with a way to
solve this problem, and I'm not at all sure what
to do."

Then he sat down beside Guenevere, placed   L-sat down beside
a hand on her arm, looked her in the eye, and   L-looked her in the eye
speaking evenly and forcefully he said, "The   L-evenly, forcefully
only thing I know to do is to tell you that you
are very important to me, that I love you, and
that just because I am away doesn't mean that
I don't care about you, because I do. Here or
gone, I think of you often. And if I could always
have you with me, I would."

Upon hearing this Guenevere's eyes filled with
tears and she embraced Lancelot. "All this time,"
she said, "I thought that you never gave me a

thought when you were gone . . . That perhaps
you were glad to get rid of me for awhile. Now
I know differently." Guenevere looked thoughtful for a moment, then snapped her fingers.
Smiling, she said, "Lancelot, do you recall
how we used to . . .?"

"I do indeed," he interrupted. "It's been
too long."   B-too long

"Well, by God, what are you waiting for?
Let's go! You know Lancelot, you're going to   B-you know, you're going
get senile before your time if you don't sharpen   to get, if you don't
up. Last year . . . ." And off they went, Guene-
vere haranguing and Lancelot laughing.   B-haranguing

Of course, from then on their friendship
grew. In fact, they were closer than ever before,
since both had learned that there was never any
reason for one to refrain from telling the other
exactly what was bothering her or what he felt.
And even though they weren't together as
much as had once been the case, now when
they did get together they took advantage of
their time to enjoy one another more than ever
before.

FOOTNOTES TO PART III

1. It can be mentioned here that the "parts" of a person
   can be characterized within a metaphor the same way
   relevant individuals can. This is a formulation strategy
   which is used in Vivace's Metaphor (which appears at
   the end of Part I and in Part VII). In that metaphor
   several of the characters are actually isomorphic "em-
   bodiments" of parts of Vivace.

2. "Digital," as used here, refers to language systems.

3. "Analogue," as used here, refers to body movements and
   voice tonality.

FOOTNOTES TO PART III — Continued

4. If he had been pointing at himself and yelling from the start, Joe's statement would have been an example of "incongruent communication." An incongruent communication occurs whenever what an individual says does not match his analogue communication, or when elements of the analogue communication do not match (e.g., a calm voice with a clenched fist). When an individual is incongruent in his communication it usually indicates that more than one part is being expressed at the same time. This is a very important concept, and it is recommended that the reader consult Grinder and Bandler's *The Structure of Magic, Vol. II* for a more complete discussion of the therapeutic significance of incongruity.

PART IV
ADDING REPRESENTATIONAL SYSTEMS

PROLOGUE

from

Cyrano De Bergerac

by Edmond Rostand

What would you have me do?
Seek for the patronage of some great man,
And like a creeping vine on a tall tree
Crawl upward, where I cannot stand alone?
No, thank you! Dedicate, as others do,
Poems to pawnbrokers? Be a buffoon
In the vile hope of teasing out a smile
On some cold face? No, thank you! Eat a toad
For breakfast every morning? Make my knees
Callous, and cultivate a supple spine,
Wear out my belly grovelling in the dust?
No, thank you! Scratch the back of any swine
That roots up gold for me? Tickle the horns
of Mammon with my left hand, while my right
Too proud to know his partner's business,
Takes in the fee? No, thank you! Use the fire
God gave me to burn incense all day long
Under the nose of wood and stone? No, thank you!
Shall I go leaping into ladies' laps
and licking fingers? Or—to change the form—
Navigating with madrigals for oars,
My sails full of the sighs of dowagers?
No, thank you! Publish verses at my own
Expense? No, thank you! Be the patron saint
Of a small group of literary souls
Who dine together every Tuesday? No
I thank you! Shall I labor night and day
To build a reputation on one song,
And never write another? Shall I find
True genius only among Geniuses,
Palpitate over little paragraphs,

And struggle to insinuate my name
Into the columns of the Mercury?
No, thank you! Calculate, scheme, be afraid,
Love more to make a visit than a poem,
Seek introductions, favors, influences?—
No, thank you! No, I thank you! And again
I thank you! But . . .

                                To sing, to laugh, to dream,
To walk in my own way and be alone,
Free, with an eye to see things as they are
A voice that means manhood—to cock my hat
Where I choose—At a word, a Yes, a No,
To fight—or write. To travel any road
Under the sun, under the stars, nor doubt
If fame or fortune lie beyond the bourne—
Never to make a line I have not heard
In my own heart; yet, with all modesty
To say: "My soul, be satisfied with flowers,
With fruit, with weeds even; but gather them
In the one garden you may call your own."
So, when I win some triumph, by some chance,
Render no share to Caesar—in a word,
I am too proud to be a parasite,
And if my nature wants the germ that grows
Towering to heaven like the mountain pine,
Or like the oak, sheltering multitudes—
I stand, not high it may be—but alone!

ADDING REPRESENTATIONAL SYSTEMS

In part I, we briefly considered the pervasive and often subtle importance of metaphors in human communication. Metaphors operate explicitly and implicitly at all levels of communication. We saw that since at least all digital communication (e.g., spoken words and written words) is *derived from* the communicator's actual experience, and since that experience is unavailable to the listener, all digital communication is metaphorical. Digital communication is literally and figuratively *a way of talking about experience*. The importance of this distinction is that in understanding it we no longer make the mistake of believing that our representation of another's experience is anything more than what it is—a *representation*.

If your representation of an event or experience varies greatly from that made by another person, then you consider that one or the other of you is "hallucinating," or perhaps "lying." On the other hand, if both of your representations are very similar, then you consider yourselves to be "in a state of empathy." "Empathy," however is *not* "identity," which is the (as yet) unattainable end point of the continuum we have been talking about. For example, a common source of ill feelings between couples occurs when one of them claims to have said one thing while their partner is equally sure that something quite different was said. Often the result is a mutual distrust of either the faculties or the honesty of one's partner. Without a tape recorder or a trusted third ear the argument cannot, of course, be resolved. For our purposes it is not important what was actually said. What is important is to recognize that one of them did *say* something and the other *heard* something different. Both of them can accept this representation of their experience (and, so, be "empathetic") without having to doubt their personal memories of the experience.

We also considered some of the ways in which the explicit use of metaphors can be used by people-helpers to aid clients in the process of making changes. One important use of explicit metaphorical communication is to employ it in helping a client recover for himself a more complete, significant, and explicit representation of the experiences he is grappling with. This new representation also provides both the therapist and the client a way of talking about those experiences which is recognizable by both as being relatively the same thing.

Explicit metaphors are also useful as a way of aiding a client in seeking and considering new choices for himself within the context of the "problem." These metaphors typically occur as anecdotes or full-blown stories which are either "true" or are tailored to suit the client's situation. Such metaphors can act as tremendously effective agents of change, particularly when they are constructed and implemented according to the models of metaphor-building as outlined here.

SECTION 1
The Representational Systems

One of the most important pieces of information that you can learn about the nature of individual experience is that people represent their experiences differently in terms of *representational systems*. Representational systems are, simply, those sense modalities which we as human beings have available and use to know (represent) the world around us. The ways in which we know (represent, experience) the world are through the sensory portals of sight, audition, kinesthesis,[1] olfaction, and taste. All of these systems are always operating. But, since much of this constant flow of sensory experience is (for many reasons) superfluous or redundant, we do not attend to it all, choosing rather to focus our attention upon the system or systems conveying the information most relevant to the experience at hand. For instance, right now you are probably most aware of *seeing* these words on this page. There is also your left foot to *feel*. And the *sounds* outside of your room. And the *smell* of the air. And the *taste* in your mouth now. Almost certainly you were unaware of some or all of these ongoing sensory experiences *until* your attention was drawn to them.

In this same way, at any moment in time, people consciously experience the world. Take a moment now for a short exercise. Write down five sentences in which you describe some experiences you really like and/or dislike. Be sure to include *what* specifically it is that you like or dislike about each experience. (For example: "What I really like about bike-riding is how relaxed I feel when I'm done," or "What I dislike about arguments is trying to see the other person's point of view.)

Now look at the sentences you have written and extract from each one the predicates it contains. "Predicates" are the verbs, adjectives, and adverbs which appear in the sentence (that is, they are words which define the relationships between things). In the two sentence examples given above, the predicates are:

Sentence #1 — really like, is, relaxed, feel

Sentence #2 — dislike, is trying, to see, point of view

Once you have extracted the predicates from your sentences, notice that some of those predicates refer to or imply certain representational systems and others do not. In our examples, the first sentence contained the predicates RELAXED and FEEL, both of which normally refer to the kinesthetic (touch) system. The second sentence contained SEE and POINT OF VIEW, both of which are visually orienting predicates. Look through your predicates and pick out those which refer to or presuppose a particular representational system. The representational system predicates which occur most frequently in any one of your sentences probably identify what for you is the most consciously significant sensory channel for that particular experience. A couple of complete examples at this point may be helpful:

Joe: I know that I should have a better grasp of the situation, but I run into stumbling blocks so often.

referring predicates: GRASP, RUN, STUMBLING

representational system: *Kinesthetic*

(In this sentence Joe is saying that he experiences 'not understanding' as a *feeling*.)

— —

Joe: On the other hand, when everything is clear to me, I can picture the whole situation, and the answers are obvious.

referring predicates: CLEAR, PICTURE, OBVIOUS

representational system: *Visual*

(Here Joe identifies his experience of 'understanding' as being one of *seeing*.)

We are not saying here that Joe's experience of "understanding" does not have kinesthetic, auditory, and olfactory components as well as visual. Of course it does. What we are saying, however, is that the portion of sensory experience to which Joe is *consciously* attending when he is "understanding" is the visual portion. If you select any discrete experience of your own (say, "curiosity") and recall for yourself some of those times when you were very curious, you will probably notice that the way in which you were aware of being curious (in terms of sensory experience) was the same each time. For example, a person who "gets nervous" before an interview might be aware of *seeing* internal *pictures* of *appearing* "awkward."

A valuable exercise is to spend a certain amount of time each day listening specifically for the predicates which you, and those you talk with, use during the course of normal conversation. As you listen for predicates you will probably notice several patterns in the way in which people use them. The first is the one we have been discussing—that is, that individuals will use different representational system predicates when describing different areas of their experience. A second pattern to listen for is that of the *primary representational system*. Just as people tend to operate most of the time out of a particular Satir stance, so do they tend to depend upon one or another of the representational systems as a medium in which to consciously represent most of their experiences. There are, then, people who experience the world primarily visually, others primarily kinesthetically, and still others primarily auditorily. That this is so will become evident to you as you keep mental track of the predicates a person uses. In most instances, you will notice that a person uses predicates from one of the representational systems in describing most of their experiences.[2]

When initially learning about representational systems many are at first amazed and skeptical that such consistent patterns of experiencing operate in all of us, and then feel overwhelmed by the seeming complexity and size of the task of discovering those patterns in others. In regards to the first reservation about the prevalence of consistent representational system patterns, you have only to take some time each day to listen to others who are conversing. Ignore the content of these conversations and listen only for sensory-specific predicates.

In regards to the task of discriminating representational system patterns, you will find that with very little practice you will come to recognize them as automatically as you now recognize idioms, for example. Like learning any therapeutic skill, the process initially involves structured and paced practice, and at times annoying awareness of the parameters of the skill being practiced. This necessity for concentration soon diminishes, however, so that you are soon able to unconsciously make and use the distinctions you need.

One thing that makes this process easier is that representational system patterns are usually very evident in the choice of predicates an individual makes. Some people literally "see" what you are saying, others are "in touch," and still others "hear you." In order to assist you in beginning to attune your ears to sensory-specific predicates, take the following sentences (which were used in Part III), and extract from each the predicates, then make a determination from those predicates of the representational system being used. Remember that some of the sentences include descriptions of more than one experience (part).

1) It's not surprising that one would feel guilt about sex, if one were confronted with such a man right off the bat.

FEEL, RIGHT OFF THE BAT
rep. system: *kinesthetic*

2) Most people you see these days don't appear as scattered as you always do.

SEE, APPEAR
rep. system: *visual*

3) I would notice a little bit of a nice self-image if I could.

NOTICE, SELF-IMAGE
rep. system: *visual*

4) I hear what you are saying, but it doesn't sound right!

HEAR, SAYING, SOUND
rep. system: *auditory*

5) A lovely looking woman does, of course, please the eye.

LOOKING, EYE
rep. system: *visual*

6) Every time I try to knock some sense into her, Joan just keeps bringing up absurd comments about this and that.

KNOCK, BRINGING UP
rep. system: *kinesthetic*

7) Why don't they knock that eye-sore of a building down?

KNOCK, SORE
rep. system: *kinesthetic*

8) Sometimes I would try and try to focus my attention on what they had to show me. You know, every time I did that, though, I became very sharp with them and cut them down.

first part:
FOCUS, SHOW
rep. system: *visual*

second part:
SHARP, CUT
rep. system: *kinesthetic*

9) If only my stereo produced as crisp a sound as those do.

CRISP
rep. system: *kinesthetic*

10) Well *I* did everything to get us all back into the picture, damnit! But that's over now. Since some individuals have shown an unwillingness to cooperate, there is no need for such efforts to continue.

PICTURE, SHOWN
rep. system: *visual*

SECTION 2
Representational Systems and Therapy

There are several advantages to being able to discriminate and use representational systems. The first is that it increases the trust between the therapist and the client, and the significance of their communications. If you hear that a client is using, perhaps, primarily kinesthetic predicates, then you can switch to using kinesthetic predicates as well ("I have a feel for your problem . . . ," "Get a handle on your situation . . . ," "That's a touchy subject . . . "). By making that switch you are operating within a world-model which more closely approximates that of your client's. This increases the trust between you and the client (you are "talking his language"), enhances your ability to communicate equivalent experiences to one another, and provides your comments with additional punch.

A second advantage occurs in relation to the construction and utilization of therapeutic metaphors. By knowing how a client most usually represents information the therapist can tell his tale in a way which is most easily comprehended and accepted. For example,

> It was apparent that the older man had seen the point made obvious by the youngster . . .

. . . is a sentence that would be most readily understood by a listener who represented visually. If, on the other hand, the listener's primary representational system is kinesthetic then the same sentence would be more easily understood and accepted in the following form:

> It was now firm that the older man had grasped the point stressed by the youngster.

The client's primary representational system, then, provides the set of predicates to be used in the metaphor.

The third advantage is that, by knowing how a client represents significant parts of the problem you as a therapist can use those representational patterns to help describe and identify in the story where the metaphorical situation is isomorphic with the real situation. Once this has been done, it becomes possible to make therapeutic changes at the level of representational systems. Suppose for a moment that you have a highly *visual* client who needs to *feel* he can "move on." Thus . . .

> And so, as the prince looked at him, he sensed welling up in him the assurance that he too understood and could go on. And he did . . .

SECTION 3
Representational Systems in Metaphor

Like Satir categories, representational systems describe one of the several levels at which people communicate. Consequently they offer the same advantages for creating significant and thorough metaphors that are capable of helping an individual effect lasting and comprehensive changes. Most people have a most-highly-valued representational system which they use as a way of consciously understanding the world around them, and through which they communicate with that world. Again, as in the case of Satir categories, the other less-valued representational systems at times become elevated to the level of primary representational system. This change in primary representational system is context dependent. For instance, a highly visual person might suddenly switch to kinesthetic predicates when asked about sex.

A frequent factor in mis-communication between individuals (or within an individual) is that those people (or parts) involved are using different representational systems in order to understand (represent) what is being discussed. For example:

> Mary: I just have to get out and do something. I feel
> (Kinesthetic)   cramped here at home.

> Bob: I don't see why. Besides, I don't think it looks
> (Visual)   good for the family to be scattered.

In the example Mary is feeling sensations in her body while Bob is looking at a picture in his head—and at that moment *both* of those disparate experiences represent "home." A powerful way of assisting two individuals to communicate who are operating out of two different representational systems is to either get them to share one that they are already using, or to get them both into a third, as yet unused, system.[3]

> Mary: (Kinesthetic) —— (Becomes) ————→ Auditory
> Bob: (Visual) ———— (Becomes) ————→ Auditory

Representational systems can be similarly used in constructing metaphors. When a client describes persons (or parts) which are significant to his problem situation, that description will often include indications of the representational systems of those persons (or parts). If the other person(s) involved are not identified as to representational system then this information can often be obtained by asking your client to quote them in regards to the situation. When the significant persons involved are "parts" of the client, the representational system of each will be evident in the predicates the client uses when talking about each of those parts.

If such a representational system switch is to be included in the format of the metaphor, when talking about or "through" a character of the story simply use the appropriate sensory-specific predicates which correspond to the representational system of the actual person or part. Isomorphism at the representational system level tremendously increases the significance of the metaphor. In order to incorporate a change in the representational systems into the resolution of the metaphor make those changes part of the connecting strategy. That is, make whatever behavioral/emotional changes which occur in the story contingent upon corresponding changes in the representational systems. In building a metaphor for "Bob and Mary," for example, their counterparts in the metaphor would be described as "visual" and "kinesthetic," respectively. At the point at which changes in their repetitive problem-cycle occurs, however, part of that change would include them "talking" with one another. In the outcome they would both be described as being "auditory."

Representational system changes in metaphors can also be used to provide a client with a choice to use a representational system which is more *appropriate* for the change he or she wants to make. Although no one representational system is inherently better than another there are some experiences which are generally better facilitated by a particular system. It is not surprising, then, that a person who represents sex visually complains of not being "interested in it." On the other hand, a person who represents kinesthetically might be at a disadvantage when faced with visuo-spatial tasks. Incorporating a new representational system into a metaphor is done in the same way as just described for switching systems. The inappropriate representational system characterizes the metaphor up to the point at which the connecting strategy occurs. Then switch to the appropriate system, making the changes which occur contingent upon the protagonist being in an appropriate representational system.

Samuel's problem is an example of a situation in which two people trying to communicate are doing so from two different representations. Samuel is highly visual, as was apparent by his use of visual predicates (he "sees" that he doesn't have enough time), while by his reports Kate "feels" neglected. The strategy selected, then, is to have them both operate out of the auditory system for the connecting strategy. Notice, however, that the desired outcome in terms of Satir categories is that they are both "leveling." One thing which is implicit in leveling is that those involved have all their representational systems open and operating. This too is incorporated into the resolution:

| METAPHOR | RESOLUTION | |
	Connecting Strategy	Outcome
Lancelot: visual-placater	auditory-blamer	leveler
Guenevere: kinesthetic-blamer	auditory-placater	leveler

SECTION 4
Son of Samuel's Metaphor

	Representational System
	V — visual
	K — kinesthetic
	A — auditory

In England, in the time of King Arthur's famous Round Table, there was a Knight of honor and greatness known as Sir Lancelot. No doubt you've heard of him. Lancelot's lover was Queen Guenevere. Now, Lancelot and Guenevere had shared many hardships and triumphs, were the closest of friends, and loved one another very much.	A-heard

In many ways they were alike, and in others
they were quite different. Both enjoyed many
of the same pastimes, and the same kinds of
foods, and both loved to converse. Lancelot   A-converse
would usually hang back somewhat during
these talks, preferring to see what Guenevere   A-talks; V-see
had to say. Of course, on the field he was   A-say
invincible But it was somehow different with
Guenevere. It was not that he had less to
say— it was just that Guenevere could be so   A-say
overpowering and hard-headed. Lancelot would   K-overpowering, hard-headed
say to himself, "It's obvious she would be glad   A-say; V-obvious
to hear my views if it was important to do so."   A-hear; V-views

One being a knight and the other being
royalty, both naturally had many duties and
functions for which they were responsible.
They saw to it that the things which needed   V-saw
to be looked after were properly taken care of.   V-looked
Each in their own way, they took care of the
people and, in many ways, were taken care of
by the people. Lancelot viewed with great pride   V-viewed
this responsibility of his, and was rewarded for
his vigilance with the respect, affection, and   V-vigilance
support of the people.

These duties did occupy much of Lancelot's
time but, whenever he could, he would spend
time with Guenevere. During his frequent visits
to the castle to see Guenevere it was usually she   V-see
who seized the initiative and decided for them   K-seized
how they would occupy themselves . . . . which
was fine with Lancelot, for he was happy just
to be with his friend and lover. These times were
very special to both of them, since both realized
that such close and loving ties between two   K-ties
people are forged by great effort and, so, rare.   K-forged, effort

Now one day it came to pass that Lancelot
was called into the presence of King Arthur.   A-called
The King looked at Lancelot with tired, heavy   V-looked; K-tired, heavy;
eyes and said, "Once again England requires   A-said
your service. You know that we are engaged in
conflict with France, and it is to those shores
that England . . . and I . . . now ask you to
travel, there to take command of the field."

Lancelot went, and was glad to do so, for he
recognized that he had responsibilities to the   V-recognized
Kingdom and to himself that in many ways
overshone those of his other duties. His greatest   V-overshone
regret was that now he would be seeing less of   V-seeing
Guenevere.

As often as he could, Lancelot would return
home to see Guenevere. But she had become   V-see
bitter over being left behind and alone. Instead   Gustatory-bitter
of the joy and pleasure of past times, their re-
unions were marred by arguments and tension.   K-tension
As the situation continued to fall apart, Lan-   K-fall apart
celot began trying everything he could imagine   V-imagine
just to please her. But Guenevere grew even
more angry when he tried to appease and please
her than when he didn't. Guenevere's usual cut-   K-cutting;
ting remark went something like, "Why don't   A-remark
you stop mewing about, eh? Any time you get   A-mewing
that bored, you should just head-on back to   K-head-on
France." Both became very uncomfortable.   K-uncomfortable

Of course, Lancelot did go back to France.
He continued to return to see Guenevere when-   V-see
ever he could, but each time he did, his eager
anticipation of his visit ebbed a little more in
the face of their growing mutual discomfort.   K-face . . . growing
He knew that if they continued the way they   . . . discomfort
had been, he and Guenevere would soon be
asunder.

One day Lancelot became weary of battling   K-weary, battling
in France and set off for another visit home.
He was disheartened and tired, and he hoped   K-disheartened, tired
that he could find relaxation in the company of   K-relaxation
Guenevere. When they were together again,
however, he could see that it was the same old   V-see
uncomfortable situation. Well, the pressure   K-uncomfortable, pressure
built-up and built-up until at last he could stand   K-stand
it no longer. He suddenly stood up, shook his   K-stood, shook
finger at Guenevere and bellowed, "That's it!   A-bellowed
This has got to stop now! This time, by Merlin,
you will be quiet and listen to *me*. Looking   A-quiet,listen; V-looking
back on it, every time this has happened in
the past, you have done all of the ranting,   A-ranting, raving
raving and brow-beating. And now it's my turn!   K-brow-beating
You sit there a moment and open your ears to   K-sit, open

what I have to tell you." Guenevere shrank   A-tell; K-shrank
back at this unexpected explosion of Lance-   K-explosion
lot's, and sat meekly while he had his say.   K-sat; A-say

Lancelot continued to pace and gesture as   K-pace, gesture
he exclaimed, "I'm not at all happy about   A-exclaimed
being separated from you as much as I am,
but I also know that what I am doing is im-
portant. And as a result we have been in a dis-   A-discordant
cordant mess." Lancelot put his hands to his
head and continued, "I've wracked my brains   K-wracked
trying to come up with a way to shed some   K-come up, shed
light upon this problem, and I'm not at all sure   V-light
what to do."

Then he sat down beside her, placed a hand   K-placed a hand;
on her arm, looked her in the eye, and speaking   V-looked; A-speaking
in even and forceful tones he said, "The only   K-forceful; A-tones, said
thing I know to do is to tell you that you are   A-tell
very important to me, that I love you, and that
just because I am away doesn't mean that I
don't care about you, because I do. Here or
gone, I think of you often. And if I could
always have you with me, I would."

Upon hearing this, Guenevere's eyes filled   A-hearing
with tears and she embraced him. "All this   K-embraced
time," she murmured, "I've told myself that   A-murmured; told
you never gave me a thought when you were
gone . . . That perhaps you were glad to get rid
of me for awhile. Now I know differently."
Guenevere appeared thoughtful for a moment,   V-appeared
then snapped her fingers. Smiling, she said,   K-snapped
"Lancelot, do you recall how we used to . . .?"

"I do indeed," he interrupted. "It's been too
long."

"Well, by God, what are you waiting for?
Let's go! You know, Lancelot, you're going to
grow senile before your time if you don't
sharpen-up. Last year . . . ." And off they went,   K-sharpen
Guenevere haranguing and Lancelot laughing.

Of course, from then on their love and
friendship grew. In fact, Lancelot could see that   V-see
they were closer than every before, since both,
Samuel, had learned that there was never any

reason for one to refrain from telling the other	A-telling
exactly what he saw going on, or what she felt.	V-saw; K-felt
Once again their lives were in harmony. And	A-harmony

even though they weren't together as much
as had once been the case, now when they did
get together they took advantage of their
time to enjoy one another more than ever
before.

FOOTNOTES TO PART IV

1. Included under the category of "kinesthesis" are kinesthesis (movement), haptic sensations (touch), and orientation information. For an expanded discussion of representational systems and their therapeutic significance see
Part I of Grinder and Bandler's *The Structure of Magic*,
Vol. II.

2. A more thorough explanation of the neurophysiology
upon which these concepts are based can be found in the
Appendix.

3. This therapeutic strategy is detailed in Grinder and
Bandler's *The Structure of Magic, Vol. II.*

PART V
ADDING SUB-MODALITIES

PROLOGUE

from

Soldier in the Rain

by William Goldman

Slaughter took a large swallow of beer and set his glass down, toying with the wet rings on the table. Clay cupped his chin in his hands, waiting. Slaughter looked across at him. Very softly, he began to speak.

"In the Pacific," he began. "In the Pacific there's a place. I saw it once, during the war. A little island. Lush and tropical. Thick with green foliage. A long white beach shining in the sun. Blue waters rolling in. Specks of white foam dancing on the sand. Overhead nothing but blue sky, stretching on and on. That's my place, Eustis. That's where I'm going when I retire. To my own little island in the sunshine."

"You are?"

"Absolutely. And the people are friendly. Kind and generous and round. All the girls are slim and round. With such skin. And bright eyes. And smiles to melt your heart. Long legs and flat stomachs and firm round breasts tilted up."

"Up?"

Slaughter nodded. "Up."

"What do they wear?"

Slaughter spread his hands on the table. "Nothing. Absolutely nothing."

Clay stared at him. "Where'd you say this was?"

"In the Pacific."

"And you seen it?"

"Yes. One time only. But that was enough. Oh, Eustis, it's a paradise beyond dreaming. And I'm going back there. I'm going back there and live like a king."

"It sounds beautiful, Maxwell. Just beautiful."

"And it is."

"Maybe . . ." He stopped and shook his head. "That's fine for you. But what about me? I tell you I'll end up married to some fat, sweaty girl and die a miserable death. I can see it, Maxwell. I know it's coming. I mean it. I'm washed up, Maxwell. You know it's the truth."

"I tell you what," Slaughter whispered, leaning forward. "Does my island appeal to you?"

"Oh, yes."

"Why, then, we'll share it."

"You mean that? You really mean that?"

"Certainly. I'll go there first and get things ready. Then, when your twenty years are up, you'll come. Picture the scene, Eustis. You standing up in some small craft. Me, waiting on the beach. The craft pulls you through the blue breakers. I wave. I am surrounded by maidens, dozens of them. In the background is the chief, arms crossed. Flowers nestle in the maidens' hair. White flowers in dark hair. A gentle breeze. The waves soften. The winds caress. The maidens dash into the shining blue water, calling your name. I'll have taught them. 'Eustis,' they cry. 'Eustis.' The sun stands still. The sky is perfectly blue. You leap from your boat. The maidens fling themselves into your arms. Flowers in your hair. Kisses on your cheek. I walk into the water. We meet. 'Welcome, friend,' I say. 'Welcome home.' The maidens begin to sing a native song. The chief makes you an offering, some gift of great loveliness. The girls lead us along the beach. The sun goes down. Soft fires on the beach. We have just finished a sumptuous meal and I retire. I bid you good night. You are alone, now. Alone with the maidens. They are dancing in the moonlight, dancing and smiling at you. They move slowly, in rhythm to some exquisite distant music. Closer. They come closer. You can see adoration in their eyes. Adoration and desire. The air is rich with perfume. Still closer. You can reach out and touch them. 'Eustis,' they whisper. 'Eustis Clay.' They begin to caress you, gently, lovingly. You close your eyes." Slaughter paused.

"That's the most beautiful thing I ever heard," Clay mumbled. "In my whole life."

"It's yours, Eustis. Yours and mine. To share."

Clay licked his lips. "Them dancing girls," he whispered. "That music. Closer and closer."

"Every evening, Eustis. Every night."

"To us," Clay said, raising his glass. "To our island! To—" He stopped abruptly. Then he slammed his glass down, slopping his drink across the table top. "No," he said. "No."

"Why no?"

"Because it's ridiculous, that's why. That's fifteen years away. You'll be old and I'll be old, too, except I'll be dead and in the ground" He slammed his bruised hand against the table, then drew it back quickly, muttering to himself. Gently, he massaged his fingers, shaking his head. "I'm going back to my table," he said. He tried to stand, but he lost his balance and fell back into the chair. "I can't even do that," he muttered. "I can't even do that."

"You don't want to wait?" Slaughter asked.

Clay said nothing.

"Well then, you don't have to. I'll share it with you tonight, Eustis. Close your eyes. Close them. Are they closed?"

Clay nodded.

"All right. Now, first you must listen for the music."

The saxophone-trumpet record was blaring again, and Clay shook his head.

"Not that," Slaughter said. "Don't listen to that. Strike it from your mind. This is soft music. Gentle, quiet music. Coming from a great distance. Can you hear it?"

"Nope."

Slaughter sighed.

"I hear that juke box, Maxwell, and that's all."

"Then try a color instead. Blue. Blue for the water and the sky. Do you see it? Deep blue for the water. Light blue for the sky. Top and bottom.

Clay pressed his finger tips against his eyelids. "I don't see nothin' but nothin'."

"Give it time, Eustis. Deep blue for the water, light blue for the sky. Deep blue for the water, light blue for the sky. Now wait. A speck of white. It's the beach, Eustis, coming alive. Stretching along the water. White as snow. And beyond that, green. Green foliage, lush and deep. And then there—there—running down the beach—the maidens. Aren't they round? And aren't they beautiful? And—"

"Up!" Clay cried. "They do point up!"

"Of course. And see how they run. To meet you, Eustis. See? Arms out wide."

"And they got flowers in their hair," Clay whispered, sitting back. "And they're calling my name. And . . ." he folded his arms, dropping his chin onto his chest. "Hey, Maxwell," he said then. "Look what they're doing now . . ."

ADDING SUB-MODALITIES

SECTION 1
The Groundwork

The way in which we as human beings experience ourselves and the world is through the portals of the five senses. We are at all times seeing, hearing, feeling, smelling, and tasting our environment (which includes our bodies), and therefore have available to us at any moment in time a tremendous wealth of sensory information. All but a tiny fraction of that information is screened-out in various ways by our nervous systems, permitting only a few bits of sensory data into conscious awareness at any one time. Without those neurological gates on awareness we would be completely overwhelmed by a flood of irrelevant information.

Conscious experience, then, is limited in terms of the number of perceptual distinctions one can make at any moment in time.[1] Bear in mind, however, that this is a limitation on *awareness* of perceptions, and that the capacity of the central nervous system to *encode and store* perceptual experience at a moment in time far exceeds our ability to be simultaneously aware at that moment of the flood of information actually being processed (see Pribram, 1971). In this process of organizing our perceptual experiences into digestible chunks a great deal of information is unavoidably left out.

Let us now apply these concepts to understanding how human beings come to have problems with various aspects of their lives (experiences). One way in which people typically organize their experience is to depend upon one or another of the sensory systems as their primary representational system. That this is so can be verified by you simply by listening to the predicates your acquaintances use in describing their everyday experiences. Or, if you prefer to be more direct, you can ask them to tell you *how* they "think." Regardless of the personal factors involved in the selection and development of a primary representational system, this reliance upon a particular modality as a medium for most of experience is a characteristic pattern of cognitive organization in human beings, and as such confers upon us both advantages and disadvantages in functioning in the world.

The main advantage of developing a primary representational system is that it has the opportunity to develop to a higher level of functioning than those not so frequently utilized. The more a particular representational system is utilized, the more perceptual distinctions it learns to make. This means, for that particular representational system, that it becomes capable of a high degree of resolution (if you are visual), sensitivity (if you are kinesthetic), or a high "signal-to-noise ratio" (if you are *very* auditory). Superior resolution in the visual system is obviously advantageous when one is involved in a primarily visual task. This gain in perceptual resolution,[2] however, is at the expense of perceptual *range.*[3]

There are three ways in which this reduction in perceptual range can help create for an individual situations in which he experiences little or no choice about what he feels and/or does (that is, a "problem"). The first is that, as one comes to depend more and more upon a particular representational system as a means of organizing experience, he becomes less inclined to utilize other representational systems which are perhaps more appropriate for some particular tasks or experiences. Thus, some people literally "*see* how they *feel*." Similarly, a person who represents primarily in the visual system is likely to have more difficulty tuning a guitar than someone with a highly developed auditory system.

The second way in which representing most of experience through one sense modality can cause problems is that important (relevant) information available through other sensory systems may be missed (that is, not represented). Frequently this missed information is of a different nature than that conveyed by the primary modality and many times contains precisely the information the person needs in order to understand and change the process which has become problematical. For example, a couple came in for marital counseling, the problem being that the husband (John) did not believe that his wife (Trudy) loved him. John's primary representational system was visual. Both he and Trudy agreed that she had many times told him that she loved him, but John never believed her. It was soon discovered in the session that when Trudy was expressing her affection for John she would "make a face" that John "saw as" a "lying" expression. The therapist then turned John's attention to the warmly sincere tonality that Trudy was using and to the affectionate ways in which she touched him. When faced with these confirming experiences John's distrust melted and he suddenly began recalling from the past all of the many kinesthetic and auditory ways Trudy had been "showing" her affection for him.

The way in which metaphors can be used to assist a client in increasing his choices about attending to, and using, other representational systems was described in Part IV.

The third and perhaps most important disadvantage of a reduced range of representational system awareness is that one is apt to miss significant *internal* aspects of experience. Problems with coping are usually based on *past learnings*. At the time each of these learning experiences occurred they were represented and stored in all sensory systems, even though the person may have been consciously aware of the experience in only one or two modalities. Each time that person re-evokes that initial experience in the form of an isomorphic experience, whether through conscious retrieval or through eliciting cues present in the environment, the initial experience will be consciously or unconsciously represented by that person.[4] This representation is associated with a "behavior" of some kind, which can also be called an "emotion" (e.g., rage, sadness, elation, fear, curiosity, and so on). And, often people are not aware of the representation with which their "emoting" is connected. Thus, clients come in and confide that "I always feel that way when I get into that situation, and I wish I didn't, but I don't seem to have any choice." Or, "I'm just down a lot of the time, and I don't know why." Or, "Every time I try to tell him that, I just can't . . . something stops me."

The following chart further describes the process of "problem formation" we have been discussing. Notice in the chart that (as has already been described in the section on "isomorphism") only the significant events of the initial experience are required to evoke the same representation and consequence in the isomorphic experience.[5] Also notice that the additional parameters of the isomorphic experience may or may not produce an emotion/behavior which is congruent with the emotion/behavior of the initial experience, and that either one of these emotion/behaviors may or may not override the overt expression of the other:

INITIAL EXPERIENCE

Parameters of Experience	Representation of Experience	Consequence of Experience
$event_1$ $event_2$ $event_3$	represented in the various and appropriate rep systems: $event_1$ $event_2$ $event_3$	Emotion/ Behavior "X"

later there
occurs an . . .

ISOMORPHIC EXPERIENCE

Parameters of Experience	Representation of Experience	Consequence of Experience
$event_1$ $event_2$ $event_B$ $event_C$	represented in appropriate rep systems: $event_1$ $event_2$ $event_3$	Emotion/ Behavior "X"
	represented in the various and appropriate rep systems: $event_B$ $event_C$	and Emotion/ Behavior "Y"

Assuming that the model we have developed for the genesis of problems is accurate there are three points in the process at which changes can be made.

The first choice that we have is to alter the parameters of the experience (that is, change the environment) so that either the contingent events no longer exist, or a contingent group of events no longer occur simultaneously. So if the cuing event is "a person," then the solution is to get rid of or avoid him/her. If the contingent group of events include "talking affectionately" *and* "making a particular facial expression" (as in John and Trudy's case), then a solution is to insure that neither of those events occurs together. Altering one's environment can be an effective strategy for change, but it is also severely limited by the two assumptions upon which it is based. The first assumption is that the contingent events are known, or even knowable, and the second is that one can sufficiently control the environment. Using our above example of the disbelieving husband, one of the cuing events may not be evident to the husband, wife, *or* therapist (such as "what she did during the day"), or the wife may simply refuse to do what the therapist suggests or what the husband wants done (recall our discussion about well-formed goals, in Part II).

A second choice we have when helping a client change is to alter the consequences of the experience, so that he no longer "feels" the way he always did when confronted with a particular group of events. Using this strategy, a client who is an alcoholic could be made to feel violently ill when drinking alcohol. Or a client could be trained to feel relaxed or euphoric when presented with a previously irritating environmental event. Or one could even not see, not hear, or not feel the event (negatively hallucinate).

The third choice is to assist the client to *change the way in which he represents the experience so that the contingent events lead to different emotional (behavioral) consequences.* As a strategy for change, changing representation has (at least) one tremendous advantage over the first two strategies: both of the first two change strategies *limit* the number of environmental or behavioral choices one can have, while *the third strategy increases the number of choices available.* By changing how we represent an experience we avoid having to eliminate or partition parts of our

environment, we avoid eliminating from our repertoire emotions/
behaviors that may at other times prove to be valuable, and we
gain new choices as to how we respond to an "old" set of events.
In order to describe how this strategy is best accomplished and
how it is useful in metaphors, we will have to descend into the
world of sub-modalities.

SECTION 2
Sub-Modalities and Experience

None of the representational systems makes perceptual distinctions at the level of the system itself. Instead, each representational system divides its perceptual organization into smaller, more
discreet discriminative units, each of which is responsible for en-
coding information along a particular dimension of experience.
These discreet discriminative units are the *sub-modalities*. The sub-
modalities of vision, for instance, include color, brightness, form,
movement, and texture. Auditory sub-modalities include pitch,
intensity, pattern, location, and timbre.[6]

When you ask someone to describe a discreet experience of
theirs (or when you describe your own), he or she will probably
first use a word or words which "stand for" the whole experience.
They feel *upset*, or see a *pair of hands*, or hear *music*, or smell a
flower. Those kind of words, however, identify only the "categories" of the experience they are talking about and are a far cry
from describing the nature of the experiences themselves. If you
then ask them to *specify* exactly what they are seeing, hearing,
feeling, and smelling, they will probably answer with a description of experience which is in terms of sub-modality distinctions.
Following are the above examples with possible specifications
and sub-modality distinctions:

Category of Experience	Experience	Sub-Modalities
I feel *upset*	I feel *pressure* behind my eyes, my stomach's *tight*, and I feel *feverish*.	Kinesthetic: deep pressure, temperature
I see a *pair of hands*	Well, they're kind of *rough* looking, *reddish*, and they're *rubbing* one another.	Visual: texture, color, movement
I hear *music*	It's *soft*, but *quick*, and it's mainly a *run* of *high notes*.	Auditory: intensity, pattern, pitch
I smell a *flower*	It smells *strong*, and kind of *sweet*.	Olfactory: concentration, fragrance

Experience occurs at the level of sub-modalities. If, then, changes are made at the sub-modality level, the experience will change as well. Schematically . . .

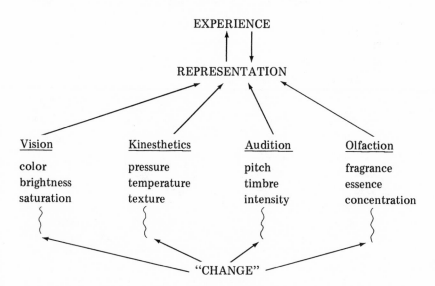

The two primary points which have been made so far are
(1) that experiences (and so, problems) are isomorphically regenerated from previous experiences, and (2) that that experience
is represented at the sub-modality level. Both of these points can
be neatly and simply demonstrated in the following way. When

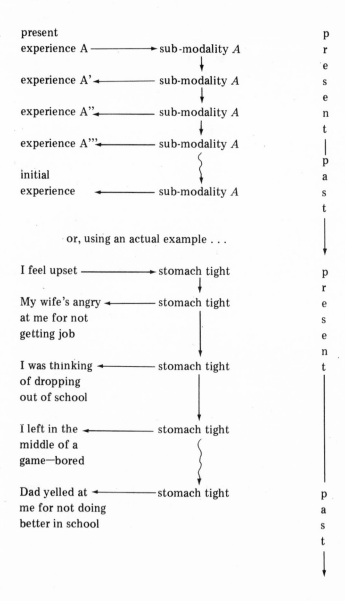

or, using an actual example . . .

next a client (or you now) expresses what, for that person, is an important emotion/behavior ("I feel upset"), ask him or her to specify the experience in the way which we described above. This will give you the experience in its constituent parts; that is, in sub-modality terms. Next, take what seems to be the most significant sub-modality distinction in the description, have the person intensify it in whatever way they can, then tell them to let that feeling, picture, sound, or smell take them back through time to an experience in the past in which they felt, saw, heard, or smelled the same thing. After each time they have related an experience to you have them continue back to another experience. When you look at the structure of each of the experiences in the resulting series you will find that *they are all isomorphic* (the arrows can be read as "leads to" or "produces").

A 30-year old woman we will call "Lily" provided me with one of my most striking examples of the ability of sub-modalities to summon up past experiences. As a participant in a training workshop of mine, Lily was exposed to the notion of over-lapping from one sub-modality to another. She was intrigued, and on her own she proceeded to try it out. For as long as she could remember she had been subject to frequent and often severe spells of "anxiety." These spells were characterized by Lily trembling violently, being flushed and in a cold sweat, and by her inability to generate internal images. Lily was highly visual, so for her not being able to make internal pictures meant that she "couldn't think clearly." Although these spells sometimes seemed to occur without apparent cause, they almost always accompanied any intrusion upon her normal daily routine. She had no idea when, where, or how this behavior of hers originated. Lily recalled the last time she felt really "anxious," intensified the feeling, then made a picture out of it. The image she saw was of a huge dark hallway with several darkened doorways along it. At one end was a lighted doorway. She walked down the hall to that doorway and looked in upon a huge kitchen. Sitting in a rocking chair in the kitchen was her very large appearing mother rocking Lily's baby sister. With this memory came a flood of others recalling to her conscious mind how once her younger sister had been born Lily was virtually never again held or stroked by her mother. Lily was so amazed at the clarity and detail of her image that she sketched it out and took it to her mother, who was mystified, since Lily was showing her exact and detailed sketches of a house that they had lived in only until Lily was two years old.

SECTION 3
Equivalence in Sub-Modalities: Synesthesia

We usually consider that each of our various sensory systems holds reign over unique domains of experience. It is more correct, however, to say that each of our senses is capable of discriminating particular domains of *environmental stimuli*. Each of the senses of vision, audition, kinesthesis, and olfaction monitor different types of environmental stimuli, but *organize that information into similar classes of experience*. These organizational classes are what we are calling the sub-modalities. The representational systems, then, are unique in terms of the environmental stimuli they monitor, but in most cases are equivalent in the perceptual distinctions they are capable of making. For example, all four of the representational systems (vision, audition, kinesthesis, and olfaction) are capable of providing information in the sub-modal classes of "location" and "intensity." If we can specify in what ways the sub-modalities of the representaional systems are equivalent and where they "cross-over," we will be in a position to generate strategies for change at the sub-modal level (which, as we have seen, is the level at which change actually occurs anyway.)

Following is a chart of the sub-modality equivalences which have come out of the research reported in the appendix.

VISION	AUDITION	KINESTHESIS	OLFACTION[7]
color	pitch	temperature	fragrance
brightness	loudness	pressure	concentration
saturation	timbre	texture	essence
shape	patterning	form	—
location	location	location	location

Some of these equivalences have been established experimentally (particularly the relationships between color and pitch, color and temperature, brightness and loudness, and for location.)[8] The other equivalences are intuitions based upon the author's experiences in using them with clients. The research includes numerous experiments in which people have consistently matched more intense sounds to brighter lights and to increasing pressure. These correspondences are so consistent that they can be mathematically described. Other research has shown that colors at the low-frequency end of the spectrum are perceived as "warm," while those at the blue end are "cooler." Similarly, the red end of the spectrum is usually associated with low auditory tones and the blue end with higher-pitched tones.[9]

Such findings are available not just in experimental journals, but these and many more are available to anyone willing to listen and watch for them in our everyday lives. Buttons connected with sources of heat are painted red, while institutions are painted cool blues and greens. Places of relaxation are dimly lit and play muted music, while places of excitement are brightly lit, noisy, and usually crowded. Regardless of whether these sub-modality equivalences are genetically wired-in, learned, or both, they are a factor in how we experience the world. In many cases, then, the sub-modalities of one sensory system directly correlate with those of another system.

The other (and probably more common) way in which sub-modalities interconnect is as *cross-overs*. A "cross-over" occurs when a sub-modality in one class becomes associated with a sub-modality in another class. Here again experimental evidence and personal observations provide numerous instances of culture-wide sub-modality cross-overs. For example: the higher the pitch, the higher in visual space is heard its source; a light appears brighter when paired with higher-pitched sounds; an object of a certain weight and visual size will feel lighter if it appears larger (the weight is kept the same); red objects feel heavier than equally heavy green objects. In our language we have "bright sounds," "soft colors," "loud colors," "colorful music," "heavy tones," and so on.

Using our previous demonstration of the ability of a sub-modality distinction to lead one back through isomorphic experiences we can now show that sub-modality equivalences and cross-overs describe pairings of classes of experience which are perceptually equivalent. Just as before, have a friend or client use a sub-modality to take him or her back through a series of isomorphic experiences. After you have three or four experiences then exchange that sub-modality for an equivalent distinction in another representational system (for example: *tight* stomach→*loud* noise; *red* → *low* tone; *cold* → *high frequency* color or tone; *high-pitched* tones → *bright* lights). Ask the person if the exchange you have made fits for them. If it does not, then ask them to make the cross-over themselves: "Now take that tightness in your stomach and make a visual image out of it . . . what do you see?" Once you have the cross-over, ask them to then use this new sub-modal perception to take them back up through time to other times when they experienced the same feeling, picture, sound, or smell. What you will find is that this new string of past experiences will include some or all of those evoked using the original sub-modality distinction, and that those that were not included before are isomorphic with the original string of experiences. This important process is diagrammed on page 121 (again, read the arrows as "leads to" or produces").

Those pairs of equivalent and cross-over sub-modality distinctions which demonstrate such experiential correspondence can be grouped together as *patterns of synesthesia.* "Synesthesia" refers to the ability of sensory discriminations originating in one sense modality to evoke patterned perceptual experiences in another sense modality. Some of these synesthesia patterns are so consistent among individuals, compelling, and seemingly immutable, that they may ultimately be shown to be a part of our genetic "wiring" (the tendency, for example, to locate relatively higher-pitched tones higher in the visual field; see Pedley and Harper, 1959). Many other synesthesia patterns are clearly learned as culturally important distinctions (for instance, the correspondence—with the possible exception of red-hot—between color and temperature; see Berry, 1961).

What has been found in working with synesthesic individuals, and what you will no doubt discover as you begin to use these

EVOKING ISOMORPHIC EXPERIENCES USING SUB-MODALITY CROSS-OVERS

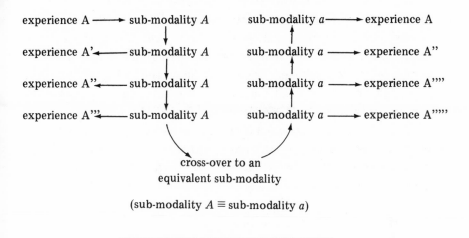

cross-over to an
equivalent sub-modality

(sub-modality A ≡ sub-modality a)

EVOKING ISOMORPHIC EXPERIENCE USING SUB-MODALITY CROSS-OVERS

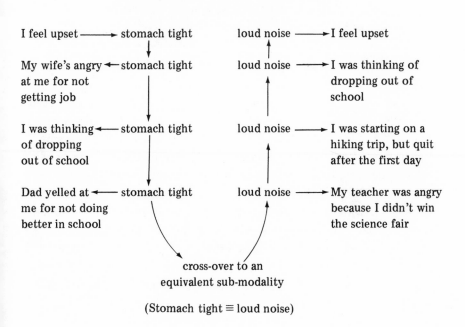

cross-over to an
equivalent sub-modality

(Stomach tight ≡ loud noise)

concepts, is that although these are synesthesia patterns which are common among most or all members of a culture, each individual evidences his own particular cross-over patterns as well. People who are labeled "synesthesic" are those who are consciously aware of vivid and consistent patterns of sensory crossing as a regular aspect of their perceptual experience. (As you have probably already realized, we are all "synesthesic" to varying degrees—interpersonal variations seem to be along the dimensions of variety, intensity, and consistency of synesthesic experiences.) What becomes evident when defining the easily accessible patterns of synesthesia among synesthesics is that, despite a few interpersonally consistent patterns, most of the patterns of cross-over are a matter of personal preference. Though subtler, often unconscious, and *perhaps* less prevalent, synesthesia patterns among the rest of us are also for the most part a matter of personal preference.

SECTION 4
Sub-Modalities, Synesthesia, and Change

Now that we have derived the concepts needed to understand how sub-modalities operate, we can take these concepts and apply them to therapeutic change and metaphors. We have already stated that experience occurs at the sub-modality level. In other words, what we call "an experience" ("discrimination," "thought," "awareness," etc.) is not a discreet and generally—definable entity, but a *person-peculiar* "constellation" of sub-modality distinctions.[10] Although your experience of "curiosity" and my experience of "curiosity" share a sufficient number of sub-modality distinctions to insure that we will probably be considering similar experiences, each of our constellations will also contain some sub-modality distinctions which are of personal significance, insuring that we will *not* be considering exactly the same experience. Since it is at the sub-modal level that individual experience occurs, it is also at this level at which lasting personal changes, capable of increasing one's choices, actually occur. Understanding sub-modalities can be used in two ways to effect such changes.

The first way in which sub-modalities are useful is in making representational system changes using synesthesia patterns for making the transition. As was explained in Part IV, two advantages of crossing-over to other representational systems are (1) that crossing-over can provide new sources of potentially important information, and (2) that crossing-over can make it possible to begin to utilize a representational system which is more appropriate for the desired experience.

The strategy for effecting these kinds of changes in the context of a therapeutic metaphor is essentially the same as that used in making representational system changes. The significant difference is that the cross-over from one representational system to the next is smoothly and comprehensively accomplished by using the already present bridges of the synesthesia patterns. One representational system is translated into another simply by identifying the sub-modality distinctions in one system and the synesthesia patterns which connect them to another system. Unlike the simple switch in representational systems presented in Part IV, translating representational systems at the sub-modality level leaves both the new *and* the old distinctions in effect. This is often desirable since all perceptual distinctions are useful in one context or another.

Following are some examples of synesthesia patterns:

1) As she looked at the red apple, she began to feel warm.

   Visual "red" → Kinesthetic "warm"

2) . . . and the louder he screamed, the brighter the sky grew.

   Auditory "louder" → Visual "brighter"

3) Soon he felt his pulse keeping time with the drum beat.

   Auditory "beat" → Kinesthetic "pulse"

4) Her perfume was so musky that it seemed to hang like a dark veil before her face.

   Olfactory "musky" → Kinesthetic "hang"
   → Visual "dark"

5) Every time she heard the raspy
tones of that trumpet, she would
recall all of the bumps, bruises,
and abrasions she had survived.

Auditory → Kinesthetic
"raspy"   "bumps, bruises,
                abrasions"

6) And each year, as his voice became a little deeper, he would set
his sights a little lower.

Auditory → Visual
"deeper"   "lower"

These representational system cross-overs at the sub-modality
level are incorporated into metaphors in much the same way as
simple representational system changes were. That is, cross-overs
in significant sub-modalities occur as part of the connecting strategy in such a way as to make the changes in the resolution at
least partially contingent upon those cross-overs. The crossed sub-
modalities are then reframed as both being important and of value.
The process is:

METAPHOR   RESOLUTION

                         Connecting Strategy   Outcome

original sub-modality   → synesthesia
distinctions   patterns ───────→ choices

A   A⇌a   A,a
B   B⇌b   B,b
C   C⇌c   C,c

The second way in which sub-modalities can be utilized to help
someone effect comprehensive and lasting changes is to use them
to help that person *change his representation of particular, significant, choice-limiting experiences.* Briefly, this process involves
identifying a particular limiting experience, specifying it in terms
of its sub-modality distinctions, then changing one or more of
those distinctions. Like any homeostatic system, the sub-modality
distinctions that comprise the limiting experience will have to alter
their relationship to one another in order to accommodate the
change. The result is a new system, which means a new experience,
and consequently, a new emotion/behavior.

This is by far the most powerful use of sub-modalities. In order to understand what makes this strategy so powerful and comprehensive we need to take a few steps back and look again at our original formula for generating "problems" (section 1, page 112), and at our formula for generating isomorphic experiences using synesthesia patterns (section 3, page 121). Combining the two, we get a pattern bearing the following form: a present (limiting) experience has as its consequence a particular emotion or behavior; since experience is the representation of perceptual distinctions at the sub-modality level, the "present experience" can be defined as a characteristic constellation of sub-modalities; this constellation of sub-modalities, if taken back through time, will reevoke isomorphic experiences with similar emotional/behavioral consequences; this process will ultimately tap the more complete representation of the initial experience. The process looks like this (read "leads to" or "produces" for the arrows):

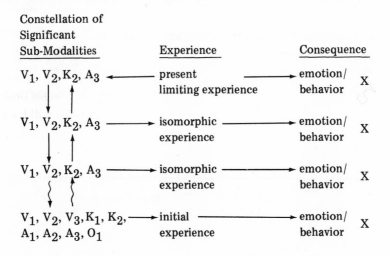

Constellation of
Significant
Sub-Modalities | Experience | Consequence

V_1, V_2, K_2, A_3 ← present limiting experience → emotion/ behavior X

V_1, V_2, K_2, A_3 → isomorphic experience → emotion/ behavior X

V_1, V_2, K_2, A_3 → isomorphic experience → emotion/ behavior X

$V_1, V_2, V_3, K_1, K_2, A_1, A_2, A_3, O_1$ → initial experience → emotion/ behavior X

Notice that our new representation of the genesis of limiting experiences implies three things:

1) Although contexts may vary, all of the experiences are essentially identical in terms of their processing and in terms of producing the same consequences.

2) What allows these isomorphic experiences to recur is the identity between the sub-modality constellations.

3) *Since experiences are organized in such a way that each generates its successor and REGENERATES its predecessor, a change in any one of those isomorphic experiences will generalize throughout the rest.*

And changing experience, of course, means changing sub-modalities.

Therefore, in one fell swoop we can change a history of unsatisfactory (limited-choice) experiences simply by changing the constellation of sub-modalities which characterize it. Like any closed system, the sub-modalities of a particular constellation are functionally homeostatic. If one or several of those sub-modalities change, then the *system* must accommodate by changing. In the same way, a star system in which one of its members changes position, disappears, grows bigger or smaller, or splits in two, will have to change in order to restore itself to equilibrium. No doubt afterwards the constellation looks different.

The problem now becomes how to best go about changing sub-modality constellations. The two primary strategies are to make intra-dimensional sub-modality changes, or to use synesthesia patterns.

Intra-dimensional Shifts

Most of the sub-modalities are actually *dimensions* of experience. A sub-modality distinction, then, is a specification of a particular position along a particular dimension of a modality. For example, "red" is viewed as being towards one end, and "blue" towards the other end, of the visual dimension of *color*. Similarly, the kinesthetic dimension of *pressure* runs from "light" at one end to "deep" at the other. Some sub-modalities may not be dimensional, but are instead made up of discreet qualitative units. Examples of these are *shape* and *pattern* in the visual, auditory, and kinesthetic systems, *timbre* in the auditory system, and *fragrance* in the olfactory system.

Making a change within a sub-modality, then, merely involves assisting a client in either moving from one place to another along a sub-modal dimension, or moving from one "qualitative unit" to another within the same sub-modality. Following is an excellent example of using this strategy:

Deborah, thoroughly acquainted with sub-modality strategies, had as a client a young man, Steve, whose problem was that he felt very lonely and unwanted when alone. Deborah had Steve specify exactly how he knew he was "lonely and unwanted" by having him check through his representational systems while recounting his last such experience. The sub-modality distinctions that appeared were that he saw himself "standing, bent over a little, arms hugging his chest, and not moving at all." His picture was in "black and white" and in it he looked and felt "cold." He also felt "empty" in his stomach. As a check, the counselor took Steve back, using his "empty" stomach feeling, to a number of other experiences, all of which turned out to be isomorphic. She then had him carefully watch his picture of himself and pay attention to his feelings, then instructed him to (at her signal) turn the picture into a *color picture*. As soon as he added color to his picture his image of himself immediately began spinning and dancing. Steve's body-feelings also changed, and he realized that he had a "million things to do" and that those times when he was alone were his golden opportunity to do any of the things he enjoyed doing. For a short while afterwards, whenever he felt unwanted and lonely, he would suddenly realize that he was seeing that old black-and-white picture of himself. By changing it back to color he immediately felt better and ready to do something. Soon the colorful change he had made generalized sufficiently so that he no longer felt lonely or unwanted, unless he specifically wanted to.

This account is a superb illustration of the main points we have been considering in this section, and of the strategy for making dimensional changes within a sub-modality. In it, Deborah has Steve *specify* his "problem" in terms of sub-modalities, then uses the kinesthetic component of his experience as a lead into past experiences. That all of those experiences were isomorphic with his "problem" was assurance that Steve's constellation of sub-modality distinctions was an accurate representation of his experience.

Deborah then selected the sub-modality in which to make the change (*color*), effecting the transformation by having Steve monitor the rest of his modalities while he changed the picture of himself from "black-and-white" to "color." The result was that he was put in touch with new personal choices regarding his emotion/ behaviors. Over the following days this experience generalized as he generated new behavioral experiences for himself and as he regenerated past experiences. How, then, do we incorporate this strategy into therapeutic metaphors?

The strategy for using intra-dimensional shifts in a metaphor is essentially the same as those already outlined, the one difference being that instead of asking the client to make the dimensional shift you *provide him with the metaphorical experience of making, and of having made, the shift.* For example, Deborah might have told a story about a young man who kept the *shades* down on his *windows* all day so that "inside" things appeared *dingy* and *drab.* One morning, while looking at himself in the *mirror*, a shade suddenly rolled-up, flooding the room with *sunlight*, and for the first time in a long time he noticed all of the *different colors* in the clothes he wore, and in his skin tones, and in his hair, etc. From this point on in the narrative Deborah would describe the changes that the "young man" experienced in his life as a result of that colorful morning. The steps in incorporating intra-dimensional sub-modality shifts into metaphors are:

1) Identify the problem, which means getting the client to specify his experiences in terms of sub-modalities.

2) Identify the solution, which is the specification of how the client wants his experience to be different.

3) On the basis of #1 and #2, select the sub-modality to be changed.

4) Incorporate the original dimensional position into the metaphor.

5) Incorporate a contingent dimensional shift into the connecting strategy,

6) at which point "change" is effected.

7) Reframe the dimensional shift in terms of the new experiences.

Synesthesia Shifts

In section 3 we introduced the concept of synesthesia patterns. Experimental and experiential evidence overwhelmingly demonstrates that our sensory systems interact at the sub-modality level in highly patterned ways. Many of these patterns of cross-over between sub-modalities are common to most human beings within a particular culture (that is, either neurologically wired in or are culturally determined). Many (perhaps most) other synesthesia patterns are characteristic of each individual operating out of his unique model of the world.

The significance of synesthesia patterns within the context of therapeutic change is that they enable us to make graceful and effective transitions from one representational system to another. Using a synesthesia pattern will make graceful and effective a cross-over from one sub-modality to another since the transition is being made by going from a sub-modality distinction in one system to an *equivalent* sub-modality in another system. The sub-modality distinctions which are used are equivalent in that, although they are not the same perceptual experiences, they are functionally the same for the individual to whom the patterns belong. We can, then, talk about equivalent sub-modality distinctions as being isomorphic with one another. That is, they function on the perceptual level in the same way as the "problem situation" and the "story" do on the level of the metaphor. As an example for yourself, perform in turn each of the following tasks, noting each time the results you achieve:

Clench one of your fists, and as you do so, close your eyes and make a color out of the feelings in your clenched hand.

Pick a color, either imagined or in your field of vision, and as you watch it, make a sound out of it that you can hear in your head.

Listen to a specific sound in your environment now, and as you listen, make that sound into a body feeling.

What you have just done is to establish for yourself three synesthesic patterns which are uniquely your own:

KINESTHETIC	VISUAL
"clenched fist"	"red(?)"

VISUAL	AUDITORY
"red(?)"	"low hum(?)"

AUDITORY	KINESTHETIC
"kettle whistle(?)"	"tension in legs(?)"

Most, if not all, of our perceptual experiences cross over in some way into the other sensory systems. How can these patterns be used in the therapeutic context?

It often happens that, as a therapist, you will decide that a change in representational system will benefit your client in some way. Suppose that your client, who is highly kinesthetic, says to you, "I really need to be able to plan ahead . . . I just keep tripping myself up." Understanding that this person pays little attention to his internal pictures, and knowing that constructing internal images is an excellent way to "plan ahead," you decide to use a metaphor to reorient him to his visual system for "planning." Using a simple representational system switch inside the metaphor may be sufficient. *Synesthesia patterns, however, not only ensure a graceful transition between the two systems, they can also provide your client with the strategy by which he himself can make, and can continue to make, that transition.* As an example compare the two following transitions based on our would-be kinesthetic planner:

(A) Representational System Switch

> He couldn't quite *grasp* what his next *step* in building should be. Then, suddenly, he could *clearly see* what needed to be done . . .

(B) Synesthesia Cross-Over

> He was stumped and stopped for the moment. So in order to give himself a breather, he laid his hands on the structure and closed his eyes. And as he RAN HIS HANDS ALONG ITS SURFACE HE BEGAN TO SEE IT IN HIS MIND'S EYE. But it wasn't a complete image, so to entertain himself he began adding to it. By running his hand along the edges he was able to mark off the boundaries in the picture in his head. In the same way he added depth. And as his fingers played over the rough surfaces, he could see the splinters, gouges, and grains in his picture. It was then that he could suddenly SEE WHAT THE NEXT STEPS WOULD BE.

The beauty of example (B) is that it includes in the form of synesthesia cross-overs instructions as to HOW to bridge the gap between the two representational systems.

When combined with intra-dimensional shifting of sub-modalities, synesthesia patterns offer you a tremendously effective way of assisting others in changing. Following is an example of how the two can be used together:

> I had as a student in one of my workshops a gentleman ("Ben") who wanted to stop feeling "anxious" whenever he would consider trying something new. This was particularly hard on Ben as his job placed him in a position of responsibility and required some creative decision-making. I asked Ben to go back to the last time he recalled feeling really anxious and to describe his experience of that. Ben described feeling "tight in my stomach and my chest, my neck's tense, and I feel pressing in on either side of my head." He had no representation

of the experience in any other system. Since he had, of course, spent many years unsuccessfully trying to change those feelings himself, I decided to utilize a synesthesia pattern and have Ben make the change in another system. I asked him to intensify that feeling of tightness in his stomach, and as he did so, to make a visual image out of that feeling. He described his picture as being "a very large, green balloon, that's a little flattened on either side." I then instructed Ben to continue to watch the green balloon and, at my signal, to make his image black and white, being aware of any changes throughout the process. At my signal Ben blinked a couple of times, then straightened up and smiled. He said that "when the image turned black and white the balloon shriveled . . . and I don't feel tense. The anxiousness is gone!" I then had him go to other scenes in his past in which he felt anxious about trying something new, had him see those scenes in color, then make them black and white at my signal. In every case his "anxiety" left him and the memory no longer held its original power over him. This new learning was then further utilized to make it a part of his future behavior.

Notice in the above example the striking correlation between Ben's feelings of "anxiety" and his synesthesic image of those feelings. Like his feeling of pressure at his temples, his imagined balloon was "a little flattened on either side." Also, the image was not only in color, but a *specific* color—"green." The synesthesia shift which was chosen for Ben was to take his *feelings* of tension in his stomach and make an *image* out of them. In making that transition he crossed-over into the two visual sub-modalities of "shape" and "color." Since the representations in each of the two sensory systems were equivalent (isomorphic) for Ben, when he changed the dimension of "color," the kinesthetic dimension of "tension" changed correspondingly. Note that there was no way to know before hand what that corresponding change would *specifically* be. Selecting the sub-modalities to be crossed and the dimensional shifts to be made is largely a matter of your experience and intuitions as a therapist and human being. In Ben's case, for instance, I could instead have had him change the "green" to "red" or the balloon to a "pyramid." We can depict the synesthesia shift used with Ben in the following three steps:

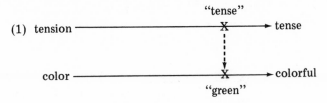

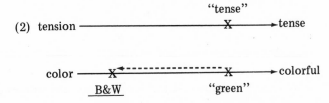

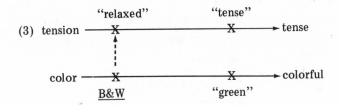

or, combining the steps . . .

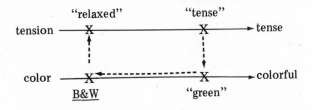

Note also that it was not only Ben's feelings of tenseness that changed with the switch to black and white. The balloon in his image "shrank" as well, while the shape of the balloon remained unchanged:

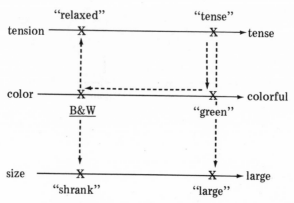

Again, when you dimensionally change one of the sub-modality distinctions within a constellation, some or all of the other sub-modality distinctions in that constellation must also change in some way in order to accommodate it. The strategy for using synesthesia shifts in order to assist a client in changing his representation of an experience is:

(1) Assist your client in specifying in terms of the relevant sub-modalities his "problem" experience

(2) Using your intuitions and experience, select the sub-modality to be crossed and the system (or sub-modality) to which it will be crossed, and the dimensional shift to be made

(3) Have your client cross-over into the new system (or sub-modality) while intensifying the original sub-modality.

(4) Have your client dimensionally change the new sub-modal distinction

This strategy is readily adaptable to use in metaphors. The steps are the same with the exception that steps (1) and (2) are taken while gathering information from the client, and steps (3) and (4)

are offered to the client vicariously through the medium of the metaphor. A brief example (Ben) of how this can be done in the body of a metaphor is . . .

> . . . One day he found himself in a very tight spot. Of course it was time for action, but he was so bound up in deciding what to do, he did nothing. As matters continued to press in on him, he began to see what a fix he was in. And as he looked at the situation, colors swam before his eyes. They swirled and danced brightly before him. Then slowly . . . slowly, the colors faded . . . faded away, to black and white, revealing to him what it was he must do. Now it was obvious what his next move should be, and he felt curiously free to take those steps . . .

The sequencing of sub-modalities in the example is:

> . . . very tight spot . . .
> . . . time for action . . .
> . . . bound up . . . did nothing . . .
> . . . press in . . . see what a fix . . .
> . . . as he looked . . . colors swam . . .
> . . . colors faded . . . to black and white . . .
> . . . obvious . . . next move . . . felt curiously free . . .
> take those steps . . .

When Synesthesia?

When a person seeks you out as a people helper he is seeking someone who can assist him in expanding and enriching his model of the world. Most problems that we humans have can be attributed to specific limitations in our individual world models. An individual, for instance, may touch a hot stove top, get burned, and then make the generalization that all stoves are to be avoided. This new addition to his world model will certainly protect him from getting burned in the future by stoves, but it will also limit him in that it precludes his personal use of a stove. This process of developing models of the world is no different than that used by the woman whose lying husband "taught" her that "men are not to be trusted," the man whose overbearing father "taught" him that "one must cower before one's employer," or the child whose constantly reneging parents "taught" him to "forget about hope." These are all recognizable to you as examples of limited models which are unique to the individuals who learn and use them. A modeling pattern which is common to us all is our individual evolution of a primary representational system and of specific representational systems for specific experiences. (I realize that everything that has been briefly stated in this paragraph has already been stated several times in previous sections of the book. These notions bear repeating, however, since they provide the very fulcrum upon which is balanced the therapeutic intervention.) How, then, can our understanding of representational systems and synesthesia patterns be used to assist others in changing?

One very useful way in which synesthesia shifts can be utilized is to provide your client with an expanded representation of his experience by drawing in other sensory systems. Many times therapeutic goals require that the client have available a wider perspective of his behavior so that he has more information at hand to use in dealing with "the problem." This is especially true when a particular problem experience is represented in only one system. We can use Ben as an example. All Ben knew was that whenever he went to try something new he began to *feel* "anxious." He was not aware of any internal pictures, voices, or smells connected with this experience of his. I felt that it would be useful for Ben to connect his feelings of anxiety with internal pictures since I already had many indications from his behavior that he tortured himself with internal pictures of which he was not aware. As long as these pictures remained out of conscious awareness they could continue to influence Ben's feelings. Once he could "see" them, however, he would have at his disposal many choices as to how to deal with them (he could change their outcome, "erase" them, make them into cartoons, reframe them, and so on.) In order to assist Ben in including his visual system in his "anxious" experience I had him make a synesthesia shift from his kinesthetic system to his visual. Once he gained the choice of making internal pictures, it became quite easy for him to connect his feelings with actual visualized scenes. So, synesthesia patterns can be used to include other sensory systems in a representation of experience.

Synesthesia shifts can also be used to transfer an experience into a more *appropriate* representational system. While there is no absolutely "right" system for any experience, some sensory systems are often more appropriate and useful for certain experiences for most people. For example, I had as a client a budding student of architecture who was also highly kinesthetic and almost completely unaware of internal pictures. His exquisite ability to sense his body movements made him an excellent draftsman and a very creative designer (as long as he was verbally describing the surfaces and "movements" of his imagined building). But when it came to drawing his creations he was severly hampered since he had no means of translating the *feel* of a building into the *appearance* of a building. Using synesthesia patterns which systematically took him from his kinesthetic sensations to their visual equivalents, he was eventually able to "build-up" his internal visual system so that he could easily represent his feelings as pictures. It was then a simple matter for him to draw on paper what he saw in his head. You can no doubt think of acquaintances or clients who are similarly limiting themselves by their use of an inappropriate sensory system.

A third instance in which you can profitably use synesthesia shifts is when you deem it useful for *two different* experiences to be represented in the same system. The "different" experiences we are talking about here are actually *simultaneous representations of polar, or at least incompatible, experiences.* When an individual tries to experience (represent) two or more incompatible experiences simultaneously, he becomes "stuck;" that is, unable to congruently put into effect one choice or the other. (Try an experiment: as you continue reading this paragraph experience being interested in what you are reading . . . and bored *at the same time.*) The point at which a person realizes he is stuck is usually the point at which he suddenly has a "problem." The syntactic hallmark of "stuckness" is the spoken or implied conjunction, "but." "I want to relax, *but* I see so much to do." "I want to love her, *but* I don't." "I know I should take care of myself so I can get rid of these headaches . . . (*but*) I suppose I deserve them." What can make *wanting to relax* and *having much to do* problems is trying to experience them at the same time. Seperately and in appropriate contexts each of those experiences can be tremendously valuable—together they rob one another of the potency and decisiveness of congruent emotions and behavior. The therapeutic task is to take incompatible, simultaneously occurring experiences and make them *sequential* so that each representation (experience) is free to function powerfully and thoroughly when wanted or needed. (What happened in your experiment? . . . . . . *STOP the experiment*! Now, what happened in your experiment? Go back, now, and find out what happens when you re-read this paragraph being "thoroughly bored;" then re-read it being "thoroughly interested.")

A consistent pattern in the way in which individuals organize polar experiences for themselves is to represent the incompatible experiences in different sensory systems. Typically, a person will "*feel* like splitting from home" BUT "*recognize* my responsibility to stay." When you then ask this person to describe each half of this conflict in turn you will hear the first described using primarily kinesthetic predicates and the second in primarily visual terms. Take as another example a client we will call "Bill." Bill's problem was that he continually "felt anxious" about all of the "things" he had to do. "Anxiety" for Bill involved a "fluttery, tense, kind of queasy feeling in my stomach." In further describing his problem he said that he felt anxious and did not want to feel anxious, but that he just couldn't stop "reminding" himself about what he had to do. When he was asked how, specifically, he reminded himself he said "by a voice I have in my head." Notice now that the part of Bill that wants him to remember things he needs to do is represented auditorily, while the part of Bill that wants him to relax from doing things is kinesthetically represented. Both are useful parts *at certain times.* (As you listen to your clients, friends, or self-described problem experiences, begin to correlate the predicates being used with the experiences being described. In this way you will soon begin to tune yourself so that in the future you can quickly recognize incompatible experiences and their representations.)

The tasks of therapy in this situation are (1) to make the incompatible experiences SEQUENTIAL, and (2) to provide them with a means of communicating so that they can remain sequential. As has already been said, what makes a set of incompatible experiences a problem is that they occur simultaneously. Perhaps you have lived in a house with other people who as a group quarreled, but as individuals, couples, or triads, lived peacefully and happily. In Bill's case, for instance, one can easily suppose that there will be times when being "queasy" will benefit him (he might swallow something indigestible or poisonous). The "voices" in his head can also be valuable, in that they provide a way of keeping himself organized in terms of required tasks. Operating together, however, they work against him. As his internal dialogue continues to remind him about his impending obligations, he gets queasy. The more queasy Bill gets, the less able and inclined he will be to fulfill his obligations. For Bill this means even more internal admonitions, then more queasiness, and so on, *ad nauseum* (literally). Once incompatible experiences have been made sequential the task is to provide them with a means of communication so that they can coordinately, rather than coincidentally, express themselves. Patterns of synesthesia allow us to accomplish both of these tasks.

Our twin goals of sequencing incompatible experiences and providing them with a channel of communication can both be achieved by putting those incompatible experiences into the *same* system. The system which the experiences are to share can be either one of those already being used or a third, as yet unused, system. In making this cross over the polar experiences are automatically made sequential since it is not possible to represent them simultaneously within the same modality (for example, try to feel "tense" and "relaxed" at the same time). Also, since the polar experiences are now in the same system they will be able to communicate with one another.

In Bill's case, for example, one part of him voices his responsibilities while the other is in touch with his need to relax. Since these two parts of Bill have previously been operating out of two different representational systems Bill has been unhappily trying to satisfy them both at the same time and succeeding with neither. However, once we assist Bill in representing (say) his "relaxing" part auditorily, the situation changes dramatically. Bill cannot be concerning himself with his responsibilities and be unconcerned about them at the same time. And, because they now share a common representation, those two incompatible parts now have a means by which they can be informed of each other's presence, and so remain in harmony. (An alternative choice would have been to provide Bill's parts with a "perspective" by crossing them both into the visual representational system.)

The basic strategy for assisting another in sequencing incompatible experiences is to use synesthesic cross-overs to either (1) shift one of those experiences into the representational system of the other, or (2) to shift both (all) of those experiences into an, as yet, unused representational system. Whenever making a synesthesic cross-over you will find that the effectiveness of your intervention will be enhanced if you select for the shifts sub-modality distinctions which the client himself describes as being part of the experiences he wishes to change.

In the actual telling of the metaphor the sub-modality cross-over is accomplished by using the descriptive changes inherent in the synesthesia pattern being used. That is, one simply goes from describing an experience in one sub-modality to describing an analogous experience in another sub-modality; being careful, however, to *be explicit about the transformation taking place.* For example:

1) And since Lisa was so relaxed, her voice was very quiet.

2) As he was always looking at red pictures, he was also quite warm.

3) Being a bell was not all that easy, for some people would pull very hard on his bell-rope. And of course, the harder they pulled, the louder he rang.

4) Neil soon realized that if he listened carefully, each note seemed to evoke a different color. The base notes were quite red. Soon he could close his eyes and watch a symphony of colors.

5) Even from a distance the shiny surface showed Lori that the thing would feel quite smooth.

6) As he gazed at the coiled hair, he wondered how wiry it was. So he reached out and grasped it, stretched it, and it was like stretching a spring.

7) He was cold all the time. He lived in a cold world which, not surprisingly, was also quite blue. But he'd been there a long time, and was now used to the blueness.

Once the shift to a new sub-modality has been made, it is usually sufficient to talk about the subsequent events and experiences only in terms of that new sub-modal description. In sentence one above, it is sufficient from that cross-over point on to talk about Lisa's reactions to her situation in terms of her quiet voice ("Even though he shamed her, she replied calmly.") At some point in the narrative her voice level changes its dimensional position to being "loud," and is then reconnected with the first (kinesthetic) sub-modality ("All at once Lisa heard herself yelling at him, and she knew she didn't want to stop—and in fact she felt her body grow more tense with each word until at last she realized that she had to do something.") From this point on, Lisa changes in certain ways and certain consequences result. Although the actual process of incorporating synesthesia pattern changes into metaphors is quite simple and direct, it is also very powerful and comprehensive in its ability to facilitate whatever potential for change a particular metaphor may hold.

Now we will return to Samuel's problem for one final revision of his metaphor.

SECTION 5
Samuel's Metaphor the Last Time

In describing the situation between himself and Kate, Samuel gave the following account:

How do you want to change that situation?

I want to feel comfortable around Kate, but when we're together she starts bickering and pretty soon I'm really mad at her. We're both mad.

What do you do when this happens and you're mad?

Well, I try not to show it because I'm afraid that it'll just make things worse.

Can you recall the last time you and Kate were really bickering with one another?

Yes. It was just last night, as a matter of fact.

Okay. Now as you review that experience again, describe for me all of the things that you felt in your body.

Well, I felt kind of hot . . . kind of flushed, and tense. And my jaws were tight.

Were you making any pictures in your head?

Uh . . .yeah. I guess I was.

Okay, describe them to me.

I just saw pictures of us finally splitting-up. We're finally so mad that we start hitting each other, and I can hear Kate yelling at me and I'm crying.

Then what happens?

Then she packs up and leaves, and I'm just left sitting there alone.

Do you recall hearing any other voices in your head while all this is going on?

Well, yeah . . . my own voice.

Tell me what you were saying, and how you sounded.

I was just telling myself to take it easy, that this'll all blow over . . . and to watch what I say. Stuff like that. And my voice is kind of calm—I guess I'm just trying to calm myself down.

In this short transcript, Samuel has not only given us a great deal of information about the progression of his problem situation, but has indicated how he experiences that situation on a submodality level. He "feels hot," "tense," and "tight in the jaws." He makes internal pictures of the two of them "hitting" when they're together, and of him "sitting" alone. And, he hears Kate "yelling" and his own voice "calmly" telling him to "take it easy." We can represent these in the following manner:

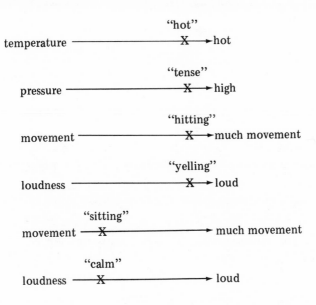

As indicated both in this representation and in his narrative, Samuel's experience within this situation is incongruent. He has been trying to be "mad" and "calm" at the same time. From his own account we can gather that he has not been very successful at being either, and is certainly *stuck* in an uncomfortable cycle over which he *sees* no control. In order to assist him in interrupting that cycle and generating a more satisfying situation for himself we will use both a synesthesia cross-over and an intra-dimensional shift.

Samuel is simultaneously trying to calm himself via his auditory system and trying to express anger via his kinesthetic and visual systems. As a result he is neither congruently calm or angry, and is helpless to change that situation. The strategy we will use here is to employ a kinesthetic cross-over from his auditory experience to his kinesthetic (using his expressed sub-modal distinctions of loudness—"calm" and tension—"tense"):

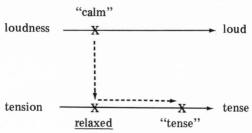

This shift will then make it possible for Samuel to alternately *feel* "relaxed" and "tense." From Samuel's description of his problem I suspected that a significant part of his problem was his lack of straight-forward verbal communication with Kate. In order to assist Samuel in expressing himself verbally we will combine the synesthesia shift we have just made with an intra-dimensional shift from *relaxed* to "tense." This shift will have the effect of dimensionally moving the auditory "calm" sub-modality distinction as well since the two are tied together by a synesthesic cross-over (and, so, are essentially equivalent.) This process can be represented as:

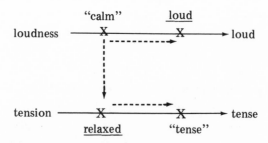

Beyond just sequencing experiences this strategy offers Samuel an opportunity to metaphorically experience the whole range of available responses in both systems. The results are a new set of choices regarding the range of responses available to him (dimensional shift) and a means of keeping those choices sequential (synesthesia cross-over).

In line with the metaphor model we have been developing all along, the sub-modality changes we have in mind for Samuel will be incorporated in the following manner:

In the body of the metaphor Samuel is crossed from his auditory to his kinesthetic system.

As part of the connecting strategy Samuel makes an intra-dimensional shift from *relaxed* to "tense,"

and change is made contingent upon his crossing back to his auditory system in the form of yelling,

so that in the outcome he has at his disposal the range of behaviors, all of which share a common representational system.

So the form of our metaphor will be:

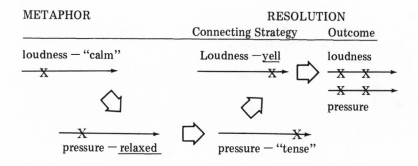

METAPHOR   RESOLUTION

Connecting Strategy   Outcome

loudness — "calm"   Loudness — yell   loudness

pressure — relaxed   pressure — "tense"   pressure

And now . . . .

Samuel's Metaphor the Last Time

Sub-Modalities
and
Cross-overs

In England, in the time of King Arthur's famous Round Table, there was a Knight of honor and greatness known as Sir Lancelot. No doubt you've heard of him. Lancelot's lover was Queen Guenevere. Now, Lancelot and Guenevere had shared many hardships and triumphs, were the closest of friends, and loved one another very much.

In many ways they were alike, and in others they were quite different. Both enjoyed many of the same pastimes, and the same kinds of foods, and both loved to converse. Lancelot would usually hang back somewhat during these talks, preferring to see what Guenevere had to say. Of course, on the field he was invincible. But it was somehow different with Guenevere. It was not that he had less to say— it was just that Guenevere could be so overpowering and hard-headed. On the other hand, Lancelot spoke calmly and quietly, and so felt at ease and relaxed. He often found his own voice soothing. Lancelot would say to himself, "It's obvious she would be glad to hear my views if it was important to do so."

One being a Knight and the other being royalty, both naturally had many duties and functions for which they were responsible. They saw to it that the things which needed to be looked after were properly taken care of. Each in their own way, they took care of the people and, in many ways, were taken care of by the people. Lancelot viewed with great pride this responsibility of his, and was rewarded for his vigilance with the respect, affection, and support of the people. He often spoke of these things while resting and in quiet conversation before a soothing fire.

These duties did occupy much of Lancelot's time but, whenever he could, he would spend time with Guenevere. During his frequent visits to the castle to see Guenevere it was usually she who seized the initiative and decided for them how they would occupy themselves . . . which was fine with Lancelot, for he was happy just to be with his friend and lover. These times were very special to both of them, since both realized that such close and loving ties between

spoke calmly and quietly, and so felt at ease and relaxed . . . his own voice soothing . . .

spoke of these things while resting and in quiet conversation before a soothing fire . . .

two people are forged by great effort and so, rare.

Now it came to pass that Lancelot was called into the presence of King Arthur. The King looked at Lancelot with tired, heavy eyes and said with a slow, deep voice, "Once again England requires your service. You know that we are engaged in conflict with France, and it is to those shores that England . . . and I . . . now ask you to travel, there to take command of the field."

with tired, heavy eyes and said with a slow, deep voice . . .

Lancelot went, and was glad to do so, for he recognized that he had responsibilities to the Kingdom and to himself that in many ways overshone those of his other duties. His greatest regret was that now he would be seeing less of Guenevere.

As often as he could, Lancelot would return home to see Guenevere. But she had become bitter over being left behind and alone. Instead of the joy and pleasure of past times, their reunions were marred by arguments and tension. Lancelot, once a picture of serenity, became over-wrought, and even became unusually rigid in his dealings with the people. With each visit home, his face grew tighter, but through it all he kept himself as outwardly calm in speech and action as he was able. As the situation continued to fall apart, Lancelot began trying everything he could imagine just to please her. But Guenevere grew even more angry when he tried to appease and please her than when he didn't. Guenevere's usual cutting remark went something like, "Why don't you stop mewing about, eh? Any time you get *that* bored you should just head on back to France." Both became very uncomfortable.

marred by arguments and tension . . .
once a picture of serenity, became over-wrought . . .
rigid . . . face grew tighter . . . outwardly calm in speech and action

Of course, Lancelot did go back to France. He continued to return to see Guenevere whenever he could, but each time he did, Lancelot's eager anticipation of his visit ebbed a little more in the face of their growing mutual discomfort. He knew that if they continued

growing mutual discomfort . . .

the way they had been, he and Guenevere would soon be asunder.

One day Lancelot became weary of battling in France and set off for another visit home. He was disheartened and tired, and he hoped that he could find relaxation in the company of Guenevere. When they were together again, however, he could see that it was the same old uncomfortable situation. Guenevere sat across from him complaining about this, and whining about that. Lancelot felt his muscles becoming taut. Then Guenevere began to make fun of him, and with each chide he felt the chords of his neck sing-out with anger and frustration. At last he could stand it no longer. He suddenly, Samuel, stood up, shook his finger at her and bellowed, "That's it! This has got to stop now! This time, by Merlin, *you* will be quiet and listen to *me*. It's obvious that every time this has happened in the past, you have done all of the ranting, raving, and brow-beating. And now it's my turn! You sit there a moment and open your ears to what I have to tell you." Guenevere shrank back at this unexpected explosion of Lancelot's and sat meekly while he had his say.

Lancelot continued to pace and gesture as he exclaimed, "I'm not at all happy about being separated from you as much as I am, but I also know that what I am doing is important. And as a result we have been in a disconcordant mess." Lancelot put his hands to his head and continued, "I've wracked my brains trying to come up with a way to shed some light upon this problem, and I'm not all sure what to do."

Then he sat down beside her, placed a gentle hand on her arm, looked her in the eye, and speaking in even and forceful tones he said, "The only thing I know to do is to tell you that you are very important to me, that I love you, and that just because I am away

whining . . .
felt his muscles becoming taut . . .
the chords of his neck sing-out with anger and frustration . . .

stood up, shook his finger at her and bellowed . . . ! . . .

! . . . sit . . . and open your ears . . . (K → A for Kate)
explosion . . .

exclaimed . . .

gentle . . .
even and forceful tones. . .

doesn't mean that I don't care about you, because I do. Here or gone, I think of you often. And if I could always have you with me, I would."

Upon hearing this, Guenevere's eyes filled with tears and she embraced Lancelot. "All this time," she murmured, "I've told myself that you never gave me a thought when you were gone . . . That perhaps you were glad to get rid of me for awhile. Now I know different." Guenevere appeared thoughtful for a moment, then snapped her fingers. Smiling, she said, "Lancelot, do you recall how we used to . . ."

"I do indeed," he interrupted. "It's been too long."

"Well, by God, what are you waiting for? Let's go! You know, Lancelot, you're going to grow senile before your time if you don't sharpen up. Last year . . . ." And off they went, Guenevere haranguing, and Lancelot laughing.

Of course, from then on their love and friendship grew. In fact, Lancelot could see that they were closer than ever before, since both, Samuel, had learned that there was never any reason for one to refrain from telling the other exactly what he saw going on, or what she felt. Once again their lives were in harmony, and he knew if, for any reason, things became tense again, that he had the resources to call a halt to their course so that they might redirect themselves. And even though they weren't together as much as had once been the case, now when they did get together they took advantage of their time to enjoy one another more than

   ever

    before . . .

became tense again . . .
had the resources to call a halt . . .

FOOTNOTES TO PART V

1. According to Miller (1956) conscious experience is limited to about 7 ± 2 "bits" or "chunks" of information at any moment in time. A "bit" of information is determined by the level at which a discrimination is made. For example, when learning a seven-digit telephone number for the first time, each of the numbers is a bit/chunk/unit of information. Once the phone number is known, that string of digits, in turn, becomes one bit/chunk/unit of information. As information is "chunked" at increasingly complex levels, generalization is gained at the expense of resolution (detail)—(for instance, consider the following levels of information: telephone book → page of telephone numbers → a line of numbers on the page → the digits on that line).

2. We will continue to use the term "resolution" to describe the ability of a perceptual system to discriminate details.

3. As used here, perceptual "range" refers to the extent of the variety of perceptual experiences discriminated. Thus, a "narrow" range might include only the visual system, while a "wide" range could include the visual, auditory, and kinesthetic systems.

4. The process mentioned here can be viewed as operating in the same way as do holograms. When a laser light is properly passed through an exposed sheet of holographic film the image which results is identical to the image which was originally recorded. The astonishing thing is that a laser beam passed through *any portion* of that sheet of film will likewise produce a complete replica of the original image. For an excellent presentation of the neuro-research supporting the hologram as a model of human memory processing see Pribram's *Languages of the Brain* (1971).

5. Events which are capable of evoking some past experiences with which they were connected are known as "anchors." These events operate as anchors in that when they occur they elicit the same set of pictures, sounds,

FOOTNOTES — Continued

5. Continued

feelings, and tastes that combined to produce the initial experience (although not necessarily with the same intensity of the original experience.) As an example for yourself be aware of your internal experience as you respond in turn to each of the following words (taking your time with each one):

Mom

Vietnam War

Christmas

As you did this you probably noticed that certain sets of internal pictures, body feelings, and internal sounds came into your consciousness. Those three words, then, are anchors for the three sets of experiences you just had. The usefulness of anchors in the context of therapeutic metaphors is described in Part VI.

6. That the sensory systems are organized, on a basic level, as sub-modalities is evident not only in introspective reports of perceptions but in our neurophysiology as well. In the visual system, for example, cortical cells have been identified which respond only to certain shapes, others only to certain orientations of shapes, and still others only to certain kinds of movement. Other cells respond only to intensity, while still others respond only to frequency ("color"). For a most illuminating presentation of the sub-modal organization of perception see Bach-y-Rita's *Brain Mechanisms in Sensory Substitution* (1972).

7. The justification for the selection of most of the terms in the visual, auditory, and kinesthetic systems is probably obvious. Since this kind of categorization has not been attempted before there is little empirical justification for those terms selected for the olfactory modality—they are, at this point, more or less arbitrary. As used here, "fragrance" refers to the type of odor (ethereal, balsamic, and so on—see Haagen-Smith, 1952, for details), and "essence" refers to the purity of the odor. A more complete discussion can be found in the appendix.

8. Example references for these relationships are:
   London (1954)—color and pitch
   Podolsky (1938)—color and temperature
   J. Stevens and L. Marks (1965)—brightness and loudness
   Held and Freedman (1963)—location
   (These references can be found in the appendix bibliography.)

9. References (in the appendix bibliography):
   Pedley and Harper (1959)
   J. Stevens and L. Marks (1965)
   Stevens and Rubin (1970)
   Payne (1958)

10. As used here, "constellation" refers to an assemblage of sub-modality distinctions characteristic of a specific experience. (For those readers familiar with Bandler and Grinder's models, what we are here calling a "constellation of sub-modalities" is equivalent with their notion of "complex equivalence." See *Patterns II*, by Grinder, DeLozier, and Bandler, and *Changing with Families*, by Bandler, Grinder, and Satir.

PART VI
UTILIZATION

PROLOGUE

from

Stuart Little

by E.B. White

"Rats are objectionable."

"I know they are," said Stuart. "But from a rat's point of view, poison is objectionable. A Chairman has to see all sides to a problem."

"Have you got a rat's point of view?" asked Anthony. "You look like a rat."

"No," replied Stuart, "I have more the point of view of a mouse, which is very different. I see things whole. It's obvious to me that rats are underprivileged. They've never been able to get out in the open."

"Rats don't like the open," said Agnes Beretska.

"That's because whenever they come out, somebody socks them. Rats might like the open if they were allowed to use it. Any other ideas for laws?"

Agnes Beretska raised her hand. "There ought to be a law against fighting."

"Impractical," said Stuart. "Men like to fight. But you're getting warm, Agnes."

"No scrapping?" asked Agnes, timidly. Stuart shook his head.

"Absolutely no being mean," suggested Mildred Hoffenstein.

"Very fine law," said Stuart. "When I am Chairman, anybody who is mean to anybody else is going to catch it."

"That won't work," remarked Herbert Prendergast. "Some people are just naturally mean. Albert Fernstrom is always being mean to me."

"I'm not saying it'll work," said Stuart. "It's a good law and we'll give it a try. We'll give it a try right here and now. Somebody do something mean to somebody. Harry Jamieson, you be mean to Katharine Stableford. Wait a minute, now, what's that you've got in your hand, Katherine?"

"It's a little tiny pillow stuffed with sweet balsam."

"Does it say 'For you I pine, for you I balsam' on it?"

"Yes," said Katherine.

"Do you love it very much?" asked Stuart.

"Yes, I do," said Katherine.

"O.K., Harry, grab it, take it away!"

Harry ran over to where Katherine sat, grabbed the little pillow from her hand, and ran back to his seat, while Katherine screamed.

"Now then," said Stuart in a fierce voice, "hold on, my good people, while your Chairman consults the book of rules!" He pretended to thumb through a book. "Here we are. Page 492. 'Absolutely no being mean.' Page 560. "Nix on swiping anything.' Harry Jamieson has broken two laws—the law against being mean and the law against swiping. Let's get Harry and set him back before he becomes so mean people will hardly recognize him any more! Come on!"

Stuart ran for the yardstick and slid down, like a fireman coming down a pole in a firehouse. He ran toward Harry, and the other children jumped up from their seats and raced up and down the aisles and crowded around Harry while Stuart demanded that he give up the little pillow. Harry looked frightened, although he knew it was just a test. He gave Katherine the pillow.

"There, it worked pretty well," said Stuart. "No being mean is a perfectly good law."

UTILIZATION

SECTION 1
Telling Strategies

Covert or Overt?

It is not at all necessary when utilizing a metaphor to try to "play down" the fact that it is intended to be "therapeutic." In fact, it is not even necessary that a client be unaware of the correlations and identities between his situation and the plot and cast within the metaphor. One of the primary functions of a therapeutic metaphor is to provide for the client an opportunity to get out of the trees and take a look at the forest he has been wandering around in. On the other hand, there is no *need* for a client to explicitly and/or consciously know the significance of the metaphor, since, if the metaphor is truly isomorphic, all of the necessary connections and changes will be occurring at the unconscious level.

Whether the client would be best served by a conscious or an unconscious awareness of the metaphor's significance will be determined by the temperament of the client and the *acquired* skill of the therapist (the nature of the problem itself is rarely a factor). Clients who manifest behavior that indicates they will be intentionally or unintentionally resistant to implementing suggested or experienced changes are probably best served by utilizing covert metaphors. It can be believed that any individual who *requests* help in changing is genuinely interested in effecting those changes. But for some individuals it is *also* easier or in some way more satisfying to thwart the counselor's efforts at facilitating the process of change.

Covert metaphors usually occur as anecdotes about "other" patients or experiences, or (more effectively) as seemingly totally unrelated anecdotes. A client with a marital problem, then, may

157

end up listening to a humorous story about the therapist's kids fighting over a turtle, or to an aside about the trouble the therapist is having getting his orchard to "bear fruit." The client who plays Berne's "yes-but" game, or who has already been to enough therapists to have learned how to beat them at their own game, or has been "forced" to be in therapy, will have few defenses against such apparently irrelevant remarks. For clients who are congruently interested in effecting personal changes, however, there is no reason (in this author's experience) to be covert in using metaphors.

The other constraint upon using covert metaphors is the *acquired* skill of the therapist in utilizing both isomorphic contexts and the patterns of experience described in Parts III, IV, and V. Acquired is underlined in order to emphasize once again that constructing and utilizing therapeutic metaphors is learned the same way one learns, say, math. First one learns the relevant vocabulary and the basic operations. And so you learn "numbers," "addition," and "subtraction." Once these are mastered, more complex operations are added, such as "multiplication" and "division." Then follow the subtleties of "fractions," "negative numbers," and so on. *Then* you get to calculus. At each step of the way new learnings are grappled with, while the previous learnings become unconscious and are handled with finesse. In the beginning, then, your experiments with constructing and utilizing metaphors will necessarily entail concentration, planning, and overt presentation. But, as these skills become integrated with those you already possess, constructing metaphors will become something you do as easily, naturally, and spontaneously as you now recall an incident out of your childhood. With this ease of construction will come the freedom to make more choices as to how to utilize metaphors.

One of the helpful side-effects of including in a metaphor Satir categories, representational systems, and/or sub-modality distinctions, is that these patterns of experience operate on a level that is so subtle that few, if any, clients are likely to be aware of (let alone comprehend) their occurrence or significance. What this means is that it can be irrelevant whether a metaphor is covert or not, provided that the changes effected on these subtler levels are themselves sufficient to effect the desired changes. This author, for instance, told a fairytale to a very intelligent and mature young man who, afterwards, said that he "didn't like it," that it was "insipid" and "obvious." Regardless of whether he ever gave the fairytale another thought or not, the changes it was intended to facilitate *did* occur because they were changes that were significant at the representational system and sub-modality levels. *The fairtale itself was merely a vehicle for making those experiential shifts.*

Fairytales or Anecdotes?

Experience shows that a well-told fairytale is as delightful, compelling, and effective as a contemporary story. Fairytales for adults need not be "insipid." Stories are deemed fairytales by virtue of their miraculous occurrences and characters, and sometimes by their ability to imbue inanimate objects with human passions. There are few people, young or old, who have not been blessed by a Deus ex Machina, or have not met a special or bizarre person, or, for that matter, have not talked to their cars. Furthermore, fairytales need not be obvious in their isomorphism, even at their most basic level of construction.

Anecdotes are merely fairytales which are usually shorter in length and are cast within the context of everyday occurrences and "normal" people. Unless you are simply using an entertaining way of putting forth a straightforward suggestion (which is often an excellent idea), the constraints of an anecdote in most cases precludes being overt.

The exception is the "My friend John . . . " approach. This involves simply retelling the client's problem (adding a resolution, of course) as though it were a problem "someone else" had and solved. For example: "I had another client in here just a few days ago and he had a similar problem . . . etc. It was interesting how he solved his problem. What he did was to . . . etc." A somewhat similar technique is to read to the client a fairytale or anecdotal story which "happens" to be a metaphor for the client's problem.

You explain that the story is something you wrote for your children (or yourself) and that you would appreciate his "reaction." If the individual is a regular client, then the story can be written beforehand (or at least outlined). If not, and you are facile, you can simply "read" from a stack of blank or irrelevant papers. These are just some examples of the many ways in which metaphors can be creatively utilized. Utilizing covert anecdotes is a golden opportunity to become flexible and creative in choosing contexts and analogies for metaphors.

One man who, perhaps more than anyone else, has mastered the art of anecdotal therapy is Milton H. Erickson (Haley, 1967, and Haley, 1973). Descriptions of his therapeutic sessions (which often consist almost entirely of Erickson telling one story after another to an entranced client) are as entertaining as they are valuable. Following is an example of Erickson's exquisite ability to utilize metaphor:

> A mother called me up and told me about her ten-year-old son who wet the bed every night. They had done everything they could to stop him. They dragged him in to see me—literally. Father had him by one hand and mother by the other, and the boy was dragging his feet. They laid him face down in my office. I shoved the parents out and closed the door. The boy was yelling.
>
> When the boy paused to catch his breath, I said, "That's a goddam hell of a way to do. I don't like it a damn bit." It surprised him that I would say this. He hesitated while taking that breath, and I told him he might as well go ahead and yell again. He let out a yell, and when he paused to take a breath, I let out a yell. He turned to look at me, and I said, "It's my turn." Then I said, "Now it's your turn," so he yelled again. I yelled again, and then said it was his turn again. Then I said, "Now, we can go right on taking turns, but that will get awfully tiresome. I'd rather take my turn by sitting down in that chair. There's a vacant one over there." So I took my turn sitting down in my chair, and he took his turn sitting down in the other chair. That expectation had been established—I had established that we were taking turns by

yelling, and I changed the game to taking turns sitting down. Then I said, "You know, your parents ordered me to cure you of bedwetting. Who do they think they are that they can order *me* a- round?" He had received enough punishment from his parents, so I stepped over on his side of the fence by saying that. I told him, "I'd rather talk to you about a lot of other stuff. Let's just drop this talk about bedwetting. Now, how should I talk to a ten-year-old boy? You're going to grade school. You've got a nice compact wrist. Nice compact ankles. You know, I'm a doctor, and doctors always take an interest in the way a man is built. You've got a nice rounded, deep chest. You're not one of these hollow-chested, slump-shouldered people. You've got a nice chest that sticks out. I'll bet you're good at running. With your small-sized build, you've undoubtedly got good muscle coordination." I explained coordination to him and said he was probably good at sports that required skill, not just beef and bone. Not the sort of stuff that they any bonehead could play. But games, that require skill. I asked what games he played, and he said, "Baseball, and bow and arrow."I asked, "How good are you at archery?" He said, "Pretty good." I said, "Well, of course that requires eye, hand, arm, body coordination." It turned out his younger brother played football, and was larger than he as were all the other family members. "Football's a nice game if you've got just muscle and bone. Lots of big, overgrown guys like it."

So we talked about that and about muscle coordination. I said, "You know, when you draw back on your bowstring and aim your arrow, what do you suppose the pupil of the eye does? It *closes down*." I explained that there were muscles that are flat, muscles that are short, muscles that are long—and then there are muscles that are circular, "like the one at the bottom of your stomach; you know, when you eat food that muscle *closes up*, the food stays in your stomach until it's all digested. When the stomach wants to get rid of the food, that circular muscle at the bottom of your stomach opens up, empties out, and closes up to wait till the next meal to digest." The muscle at the bottom of your stomach—where's the bottom of your stomach when you're a small boy? It's all the way down.

So we discussed that for an hour, and the next Saturday he came in all alone. We talked some more about sports and this and that—with never a mention of bedwetting. We talked about Boy Scouts and camping, all the things that interest a small boy. On the fourth interview he came in wearing a big, wide smile. He said, "You know, my Ma has been trying for years to break *her* habit. But she can't do it." His mother smoked and was trying to stop. I said, "That's right, some people can break their habits quickly, others make a great big talk about it and don't do nothing about it." Then we drifted on to other subjects.

About six months later he dropped in socially to see me, and he dropped in again when he entered high school. Now he's in college.

All I did was talk about the circular muscle at the bottom of the stomach closing up and holding the contents until he wanted to empty it out. Symbolic language, of course, but all that beautiful build-up of eye, hand, body coordination. The bedwetting went away without ever discussing it.

(from Haley, *Uncommon Therapy*, pp. 199-201)

Notice that in his metaphor Erickson uses both a synesthesia cross-over and a dimensional shift within the metaphor in order to teach the boy about "closing down." I heartily recommend that you peruse transcripts and reports of Erickson using metaphors since they are excellent examples of multi-level, comprehensive, and effective therapeutic interventions. They provide an indication of the range of variety and versatility of metaphorical communication, and they are very definitely fun.[1]

Quotes

"What," you wonder, "is he referring to when he talks about 'quotes'?" I answer, "Well, once I was putting someone into a trance, and as I continued to do so, I said to that person, 'You *can* feel the tremendous need to *blink.*'"

"Now wait a second. When you said, 'blink' I blinked!"

"That's right."

"I'm beginning to understand. I can covertly make direct suggestions and statements to my client—or anyone—simply by dressing the statement up as a quote made by someone else!"

"Right. At times you may want to make a direct statement to your client without your having to claim personal responsibility for the statement's content. For instance, suppose you are my boss and a Simon Legree to boot. If I were to say to you—Boss, you're a louse!—you would no doubt get angry and sack me on the spot. If, however, I casually said—Boss, a man just came into my office and gave me a hard time, so I said to him, 'You know, you're a louse!'—I still have the satisfaction of calling you, the Boss, a louse, the Boss has had the experience of being called a louse, *and* it wasn't me saying it to him—I was saying it to that 'man.'"

"Ahh. So then the point is that my client can argue with and discredit statements *I* make, but can do nothing about things 'someone else' said."

"Exactly so."

"And so, in the context of metaphors, I can simply have the characters in the story say to my client what it is I, as a therapist, want to say. For example, I might say something like 'This fella handed me a whole stack of papers on which he had written alot, I mean aaa-lot, of words. He was smirking just a little, so I read through those pages quickly, then, looking up at him, asked if this was all there was . . . . . He didn't answer—just looked surprised—and I said to him, "You know, I've known all this stuff in one form or another for a long time. For an author you're not too bright, are you?"'"

"You got me."

"Natch."

Hypnosis

One of the attributes that distinguishes hypnosis is that it is an excellent state of consciousness in which to learn. While in trance, most people are remarkably receptive to new ideas and are often in command of much more personal information than usual regarding their past experiences and present awarenesses. This makes trance an ideal situation in which to use metaphors since the resulting transderivational searches are likely to be more thorough, and the resolution more likely to be integrated. When using metaphors (particularly fairytales), this author frequently induces a light or medium trance in the client (with permission of course) as a prelude to the story-telling. Although certainly not necessary, if you are qualified to do hypnosis and if the client is willing, story-telling and trance can provide you with a powerful therapeutic process. Another, not-to-be overlooked advantage of having the client in trance is that it frees you to take your time with constructing and unfolding the metaphor (the period of time while your client is putting himself "deeper into trance" is often a good time to sit back and plan your metaphor).

You should also realize that the very act of telling a story (fairytale or anecdote) is somewhat mesmerizing. The process of internally representing a relatively unfamiliar sequence of events, of attending closely to the communications of another person, and of anticipating the succession and resolution of events, can be deeply hypnotic. This effect is compounded by the use of the communication pattern distinctions described in Part II. Those distinctions comprise some of the basic communication patterns used in hypnosis. The patterns of deletion, unspecified verbs, and nominalizations, are used to maximize for the client the extent of their reliance on transderivational phenomena, ensuring the significance and thoroughness of the metaphor. This also means that, when telling a fairytale or anecdote to an originally "normal" client, that client may become somewhat "trancy;" that is, quiet, relaxed, and apparently either very attentive or very preoccupied. This is a state we all experience periodically, is advantageous for the previously mentioned reasons, and provides an opportunity for the therapist to utilize metaphors in different ways.

Calibration

What allows a metaphor to be significant, comprehensive, and effective is that it is an isomorphic representation of the client's problem situation. In other words, a therapeutic metaphor is an analogy which is as detailed and as equivalent to a problem situation as is practical. Much of this book has been devoted to providing you with the skills necessary to insure that your metaphors *are* isomorphic representations on all the levels at which they operate. As a fellow human being and people-watcher perhaps you have already developed yet another skill which is valuable, if not essential, in utilizing metaphors—the ability to intentionally calibrate your own behavior from the behavior of another person.

The term "calibration" was introduced in Part II as a description of the *unintentional* emotion/behavior loops people get into. The term has the same definition here, with two exceptions: we are specifically applying it to communication between two individuals; and, we are *intentionally* using it as a tool. The use we are putting it to here is as *a means of knowing from moment to moment whether or not a metaphor is indeed significant and comprehensive for the client.* "Am I getting through?" is the question we are answering.

Whenever you communicate with another person you consciously or unconsciously monitor their reactions to what you are saying and doing. If they suddenly appear disgusted, you might change your topic; if they appear confused, you might repeat or expand what you have said; if they appear attentive, you will probably continue. You are, then, calibrating your behavior from that of the other person. When telling a metaphor to a client, regardless of whether he is in a trance or awake, it is important to monitor his reactions to the tale as it progresses. A client's facial changes, skin tone changes, body movements and positioning, and sometimes vocalizations, will all provide you with constant feedback as to when and where the story becomes confusing, off-the-mark, not appreciated, or the reverse of those. When a compressed brow tells you that you are not being sufficiently clear, or a wrinkled nose tells you that you have made an incorrect association, use that indicator to make whatever changes you think that you need to make in the narrative. In the same vein, skin flushes, a tear, or a smile can also indicate to you possible bull's-eyes—associations which you can then expand on if appropriate.

Guided Fantasies

One possibility for constructing and using metaphors is to have the *client* do the work. It is undeniable that no one could construct for another individual a metaphor as meaningful as the one which that person constructed for himself. This, then, is a "guided fantasy," in which a client pursues some fantasy of his own choosing and is directed by the therapist's comments and questions to attend to potentially significant aspects of the fantasy. The technique has some seniority by now, and is described in detail elsewhere.

The subject of guided fantasies is brought to your attention here not only because it is obviously a utilization of metaphor, but because by using the skills you are acquiring here the technique is rendered much more sophisticated in terms of what can be done with it and through it. By understanding Satir categories, representational systems, and sub-modality patterns, the fantasy "guide" is alerted to patterns of experience expressed on those subtle levels. He is also in a position, as a knowledgeable guide, to direct the client's attention to these patterns, and to then assist him in making appropriate changes in those patterns.

A way of utilizing metaphors which bears some kinship with guided fantasies is to turn over the responsibility of *resolving* a therapist-constructed metaphor to the client. Depending upon the nature of the problem and the client's temperament, he could be asked to "finish" (i.e., resolve) a metaphorical fairytale begun by the therapist. (These approaches are particularly effective with children since they are usually very attentive to stories, readily accept the reality of the characters, and easily generate creative resolutions.) The "My friend John . . ." approach is particularly suited to this type of utilization. Using it, the therapist can simply describe to the client the situation of "another" client or friend who has an isomorphic, "similar," or even "identical" problem. Feigning ignorance of what to do (which, considering the present client, may not be a feign), he then asks the client what he would do about the situation. If the client has an answer it will be a veritable blueprint for solving his own problem situation since that answer had to come from his own model of the world. In fact, it may not even be necessary to develop that blueprint, since often the client consciously or unconsciously realizes that he has just been the architect of a solution for his own problem.

SECTION 2
Anchors and Triggers

Anchors

Everyone has periodically had the experience of seeing, hearing, feeling, smelling, or tasting something which immediately takes them back to some experience or event in the past. Perhaps you happened to catch the fragrance of a flower that suddenly brought to mind a girl you hadn't thought of in years; or your boss pointing his finger and yelling at you put you in mind of being a kid again and in trouble with Father; or walking on sand takes you back to that "time" with that "guy;" and, of course, all of the Christmases that take you back rummaging among all of the other Christmases. These bits of experience are *anchors* for larger, past, and often otherwise forgotten, experiences. In our examples the anchors are a flower fragrance, a scene and a tonality, the feel of sand, and a particular holiday. These anchors for past experiences are, of course, essentially sub-modal representations and constellations of those representations which are capable of turning you to leaves from the pages of your past. Sometimes pictured, recorded, or embossed upon those leaves are pleasant and/or useful experiences. At other times the anchor dredges up experiences which are not only painful, but are no longer useful either. Another thing which is significant about anchors is that, *though they are discreet perceptions, one does not have to be consciously aware of them in order for them to function.* Anchors are cuing each and every one of us back to prior experiences throughout the day. Many of the daily sensations and perceptions we experience and necessarily ignore happen to be discreet members of sub-modality constellations representing various past experiences. And so, we sit at the table and suddenly recall "that trip back," unaware that a plane has just audibly passed overhead. Or we recall an evening of chips-and-dip with friends, unaware (or not connecting the fact) that someone has just crushed a paper bag. Or we suddenly feel melancholy and don't know why, while unnoticed by us there is a woman weeping on the kid's television. Anchors can provide a way of quickly returning us to past emotion/behaviors, and often provide us with pleasant and stimulating surprises. They can also continue to evoke past emotion/ behaviors which are now inappropriate or painful. How to go about "pulling-up" those unwanted anchors has been the main topic of this book.

On the other hand, anchors can be *intentionally* used to increase the effectiveness of therapeutic metaphors. In order for an individual to describe an experience he must first represent it in one or more of the sensory systems. When that person is representing an experience (as, say, a "memory") he *is experiencing that experience on some level* since "representation of experience" and "experience" are identical processes. *Therefore, when an individual is describing some personal experience, he is, in some measure, actually re-experiencing the emotion/behaviors being reported.* What the client is reporting is a constellation of sub-modality distinctions, each of which is capable of acting as an anchor for the entire set (experience). When you perceive (via the client's appearance, tonality, and words) that the client is as fully "back" into the experience as he goes, you can *take that opportunity to anchor the experience yourself by introducing some discreet sub-modality-level sensation into the constellation.* You could, for example, squeeze his knee, or make a discreet noise (like a sniff, a lip smack, or a rap on the table), or change your tonality, or (if you will be maintaining visual contact) you can make an obvious and discreet body or facial movement, such as leaning foreward or frowning.

Once these anchors have been repeated once or twice they acquire the ability to *evoke* the anchored experience, just as did any of the original "anchors." The response to "firing-off" (using) the anchor may be minimal, but it is nonetheless there exerting some influence over the whole of the client's experience.

What is significant about these newly created anchors is that *they are under the control of the therapist.* While the client is describing each of the experiences relevant to his problem, the therapist sets up anchors for each one over which he would like some evocative control. Each time the client congruently expresses one of those experiences, the therapist repeats his anchor so as to insure its inclusion in that sub-modality constellation.[2] As a therapist, this can be useful to you in utilizing metaphors in that, once the anchors are "set," by selectively firing them off you can help to insure that the client is "fully experiencing" those parts of the metaphor which are isomorphic with the anchored emotion/behaviors.

Let us take Samuel's problem for an example. To begin with, we could *sniff* each time Samuel describes his extra-relationship responsibilities, and *cluck tongue* each time he talks about his helplessness at home. With a little foresight, we can also ask him about some of his really good times with Kate, and anchor those with a *squeeze of his knee.* During the course of telling Samuel his tale, each time we describe Lancelot's knightly responsibilities we insert a *sniff* or two. In the parts where Lancelot is confronted with Guenevere's anger, at an appropriate place, we insert a *tongue cluck*. The purpose of firing-off these anchors is to facilitate Samuel in his making personally significant meaning out of the metaphorical events he is hearing and witnessing. Having had the foresight to anchor a pleasant experience before commencing the tale, we can now reach over and *squeeze* Samuel's *knee* as we describe Lancelot and Guenevere's reunion.

Anchors can also be used to *integrate* (and, so, defuse) incompatible emotion/behaviors. In this case, the anchors are used in precisely the same way and on the same occasions as described above. The difference is that at the point in the metaphor where change occurs (the connecting strategy) both anchors are fired-off *simultaneously*. In Samuel's metaphor, then, we would *cluck* and *sniff* simultaneously (try it . . . very interesting) at the point at which Lancelot at last integrates the two experiences (after having changed the way in which he communicated with Guenevere.) The result is that Samuel's two supposedly polar experiences of being "responsible" and being "helpless" are forced to collapse into a new experience which combines the most useful aspects of each of its precursors. This strategy can be represented as . . .

THIS

METAPHOR	RESOLUTION	
	connecting strategy	outcome

What is important to notice about this strategy is that *at the point at which change is occurring the two incompatible emotion/ behaviors are forced to simultaneously manifest themselves.* Since they cannot occur simultaneously they are compelled to break-apart and reform a single, new constellation of sub-modalities. This new constellation (experience) will necessarily be made up of compatible sub-modal perceptions from each of the two original sets. From that juncture on, the original anchors (sub-modal perceptions) that comprised each of the original experiences will no longer evoke those experiences, since they no longer exist as that original set of sub-modalities. (Try it—after you have collapsed two incompatible experiences, fire each of the anchors individually and notice whether or not you get the original responses.)

Triggers

Anchors and triggers are actually two reciprocal parts of the same process. Whereas an "anchor" is an individual's perception of an environmental event, a *"trigger" is the environmental event itself.* Thus, in the above example, the sniff and the squeezing hand are triggers, while Samuel's auditory perception of that sniff and his kinesthetic perception of that hand-squeeze are anchors. Although anything can act as a trigger, environmental events are not triggers unless they anchor some particular experience. This distinction is important as it alerts us to the fact that recurrent environmental events are an inseparable part of emotion and behavior. As discussed in Part II, when a coping problem arises we can change either the environment (the triggers), the experience of the environment (the anchors), or the consequent response. Although effecting changes at any one of these levels will generalize throughout the other two, for reasons already covered, we determined that working with a client at the level of his experience of the world is the most viable choice in most cases.

There are, however, ways in which the use of triggers can be incorporated into metaphors, and therapy in general, to facilitate changing. The first of these is to *switch the trigger of an unpleasant emotion/behavior to triggering a pleasant or more useful experience.* When a client is specifying the characteristics of a problem situation for you, frequently you will notice that there is one particular environmental event (trigger) which is always effective in, if not solely responsible for, eliciting that experience. Such triggers could be a pointing finger, a harsh voice, the name of a person, the throb of a war wound, the smell of a pipe, and so on. Assuming that the trigger you are considering is responsible for eliciting an unpleasant (or at least not helpful) emotion/behavior, then one way in which to change that situation is to make that the same trigger for a different experience.

Changes in trigger reference are easily included in metaphors. To do this, take the trigger that the client has indicated as being most or solely evocative of his problem situation and incorporate it into your metaphor in the same functional position as it had in the "real" situation. After the metaphorical characters have made their changes, *reframe the previously troublesome trigger as a future trigger for the changes that have just been made.* For example: "From that day on, *whenever Willi's boss raised his voice it reminded Willi* of this special experience through which he had learned so much about lonely people who yell . . . " (italicized words indicate tonal emphasis). This brief moment spent reframing a trigger forges a powerful tool for the client as it provides him with a means of immediately returning to a relevant learning experience at precisely the time at which he needs to.

The triggers we have just been talking about are not under the control of the therapist. Such triggers, and triggers which *are* under the control of the therapist, *can also be used to initiate changes at appropriate times in the future.* It may be that the nature of the client's problem indicates that the actual process of changing would be best facilitated if it occurred within the context of the actual problem situation. In this case, all that is needed is for the therapist to select as a trigger one of the various environmental events which *characterize* the client's actual problem situation, and then explicitly incorporate it as a *trigger for the changes* that occur in the metaphor. For example: "And it was not until later when the young man *pointed at him* that *Willie realized* the significance of what he had learned. The young man *pointing at him caused everything that had gone on before* to fall into place, so that Willi could begin to change . . . " In this way the stage is set for the client to return to his problem situation with a trigger for changing. When that trigger is pulled, he can begin to make changes in accordance with the suggestions in the metaphor. The difference is that those changes are being made within (*and with respect to)* the context of the actual problem situation. Of course, as the therapist, you can also establish triggers over which you have control so that you can initiate changing at subsequent and, perhaps, more appropriate times (for an example, see Vivace's *Metaphor And The Tale of Two Hiccups* in Part VII).

SECTION 3
STACKING REALITIES

The "reality" we are referring to here is that group of awarenesses which occurs within the same environment in which you are now reading this book, as revealed to you through your five senses, constitutes a reality. All of the external events you now perceive as you monitor your environment intuitively seem to be equally "valid," or "concrete," or "compelling," or "apparent," and so on. What is important for our purposes here is to recognize that we can discriminate between the reality of this page and, say, the reality of your internal fantasy world. We do not need to agree on what are the specific differences between those two realities in order to agree that they are indeed "somehow" different.

Stacked realities refers to experiences which are simultaneously represented at more than one level of meaning. As an illustration of stacking realities, let us take the word "dog." One reality that is available to you through your eyes is the printed configuration DOG. If you then make an image in your head of a "DOG" you have added a second reality. Now imagine a child who is imagining a "DOG," and you have just stacked three realities—one on top of the other. Throwing in the fact that you are also reading this in a particular environment, you are now stacking at least four realities . . . and so it goes. (The concept of stacked realities always reminds me of the painting of a wall on which hangs a painting of a wall on which hangs a painting of a wall . . . .) What makes this concept useful is the recognition that people represent much of their experience at various levels of reality, and that any one of those levels of reality is as faithful a representation of experience as the next. It is precisely this equivalence of realities which enables therapeutic metaphors to operate as effective agents of change (and, incidentally, enables you to understand this page of hieroglyphics). As you may have already realized, whenever you tell a fairytale or anecdote you are stacking at least three realities: the reality of your talking with the client within certain physical surroundings, the reality of the client's representation of his problem, and the reality of the client's representation of the metaphor for his problem.

The advantage of understanding the concept of stacked realities is that it frees you to intentionally and simultaneously operate on several levels of awareness when working with a client. Because perceptual experience is relatively unlimited while conscious experience is, therapeutic communications which operate at several levels of reality are virtually irresistable. As an example, recall from the first section the case-example of the young man who "didn't like" the fairytale told to him. He was able to dismiss the reality of the metaphor's plot as "insipid," but he was unable to dismiss the realities of the representational system and submodality changes contained within the metaphor. They operated at a level of reality of which he was not aware.

If you happen to be present when a client is involved in an actual situation which is isomorphic with, or identical to, the problem situation, you have the opportunity to make what is one of the most effective uses of metaphors. That is, since the client will be involved in an example of the experience he wants to change, he will have the opportunity to put into immediate effect the suggestions contained in your anecdote. The changes that result can then be further utilized by you right at the time. Following is an excellent example of stacking realities in this way:

> Deborah (who was trained in the use of metaphors) was out to dinner with two new acquaintances, Tom and Samantha. Samantha was a grade school teacher, and did not know that Deborah

knew that. It was quite obvious that Samantha took it upon herself to continually tell Tom what to do. When their party arrived at the restaurant, Samantha, with her usual brusque manner, said to Tom, "You can take your coat off, you know." Then, in a joking manner, Deborah said to Tom, "I'll bet you didn't know that." Tom, who normally obeyed Samantha, came out of his routine for a moment and realized how mindlessly he had been trudging in whatever direction Samantha aimed him. There followed an argument between Samantha and Tom, during which Tom asserted himself. Their confrontation left a bitter taste in their mouths, however, since neither one of them understood how they had come to establish a relationship in which Samantha took responsibility for Tom's actions.

While eating dinner later that evening, Deborah told a short anecdote about a friend of hers who was a teacher. This friend spent so much time with kids all day, that often she found herself talking to adults as though they were children—and she hadn't meant to. Samantha blinked a few times, then said, "You know, *I'm* a school teacher, and *I* think I do that too . . . " From that point on, it was clear to both Samantha and Tom how their routine had originated, and both were relieved to know that it was not the product of her "need to dominate" and/or his "need to submit."

One additional thing which can be profitably pointed out about this anecdote is the way in which *response potential* was built up. By waiting for awhile after the initial confrontation, Deborah allowed Samantha and Tom time during which they almost certainly searched inside themselves for a way to understand what was happening between them. Since their searching was in vain their readiness to respond to a likely possibility was no doubt higher than it would have been before or during the argument (when the "likely possibility" would probably have been taken as "information," rather than as "revelation"). By using a metaphor Deborah also provided them with the opportunity to realize their own solution to their problem.

In section 1 we discussed the use of quotes as a way of covertly stepping out of the metaphor to make direct statements to a client. In using quotes you are actually stacking realities. In its simplest form, when telling a metaphor containing quotes there is (1) the reality of you talking to your client within your office, (2) the reality of the story's isomorphism, (3) the reality of the direct statements (quotes) to your client, and (4) the reality of your client's internal representation of the first three.

Similar to quotes, we can also finger "organ language" as a means of stacking realities. "Organ language" refers to all of the words in our language which serve multiple duty as names of parts of our anatomy or physiological functions and as descriptions of other experiences. For instance, suppose I said to you, "Give me a hand." Unless you know the context of the statement, "hand" could refer to a piece of anatomy, some assistance, or applause. In the same way you can use organ language to make statements which are significant on more than one level. To a client whose problem was chronic nausea you could make statements which included a phrase like, ". . . could not *stomach* . . . " Similarly, people "have a lot of *gall*," "give *thumbnail* sketches," "get *pissed* off," "are *heels*," "gird their *loins* and *arm* themselves," are *"nosey," "tongue* tied," and *"cheeky,"* need *elbow* room," "give *lip* service," and "have *heart."* Organ language is especially useful in telling metaphors designed to aid a client with a problem which manifests itself as some form of physiological disorder.

Analogue marking is another one of the tools that will enable you to stack realities in addition to those inherent in the metaphor. As explained in Part II, analogue marking involves emphasizing particularly important concepts in a communication by specific changes on the part of the therapist in voice tonality, in appearance, or in physical contact. When telling a metaphor, these analogue signals can be used to characterize different aspects of the tale. For instance, within the same story one could use a harsh tonality when talking about the protagonist's encounters with troubles, a low-pitched tonality when considering hopes and dreams, and a high-pitched tonality when considering changes. This is what excellent story-tellers have always done. *Analogue marking the different aspects of the metaphor creates another reality in which the story is "told" in terms of an isomorphic pattern of analogue cues.*

Analogue marking and stacked realities can also be used when telling multiple metaphors (that is, several metaphors about the same problem). Suppose a client comes in and describes the following (simplified) problem: "Every time I go to take a test, I blow it. I know the material, but when I get to the class I start worrying that maybe I don't. Pretty soon, I get so nervous and panicky that I don't remember a thing, and I either have to leave, or, if I stay, flunk the test." This problem could be divided into the following "events" ("units," "stages," "TOTEs,"[3] etc.):

Problem Events

I	II	III	IV	V
knows material	doubts ability when gets to class	panics and forgets	leaves and/or fails	(no resolution)

One technique for using metaphors is to take a problem, such as above, and tell several short anecdotes, all of which are isomorphic with the problem. What makes this technique effective, however, is the use of analogue marking of each of the problem units. This is done (1) by telling as many anecdotes as there are problem-events, and (2) by sequentially analogue marking (*with the same cue*) in each of the anecdotes one of the problem events. In other words, in our above example, the first event would be marked in the first anecdotes; the second event would be marked *in the same way* in the second anecdote; the third in the third, and so on. The process looks like this:

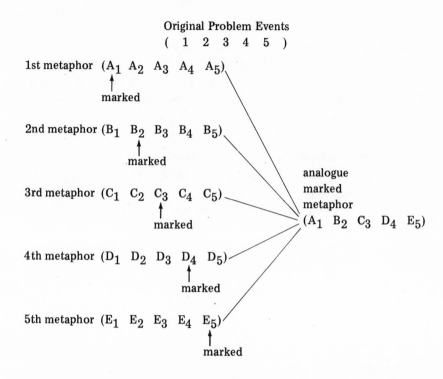

By analogue marking in this manner, each of the events that are marked with the same cue will be unconsciously associated with one another. When at last the resolution event is marked, the client will have unconsciously represented a *sixth* metaphor which was "collapsed" out of the previous five.

FOOTNOTES TO PART VI

1. You are particularly encouraged to read Parts I and II of Erickson's article entitled, "A Study of an Experimental Neurosis Hypnotically Induced in a Case of Ejaculatio Praecox," which can be found in *Advanced Techniques of Hypnosis and Therapy* (Jay Haley, ed.). In that article you will find all of the patterns presented here coupled with Erickson's unique ability to organize and utilize those patterns.

FOOTNOTES — Continued

2. It is usually necessary to anchor an experience only once or twice (provided that you have timed your anchoring to coincide with the experience when it was at its strongest). If you have any doubts, merely fire off the anchor at an inocuous moment and notice whether or not you get the expression of some of the analogue cues present in the originally anchored experience.

3. "TOTE" (which stands for Test Operate Test Exit) is Miller, Galanter, and Pribram's name for the basic unit of perceptual or behavioral processes (1960). The point of it and the other words used to indicate the segments of a "problem" is that problems are processes which can be segmented into naturally occurring steps in order to make them more accessible and understandable—call them what you will.

PART VII
EVERYTHING, ALL AT ONCE, TOGETHER

PROLOGUE

from

The Once and Future King

by *T. H. White*

"How does one get hold of a sword?" he continued.
"Where can I steal one? Could I waylay some
knight even if I am mounted on an ambling pad,
and take his weapons by force? There must be
some swordsmith or armourer in a great town like
this, whose shop would be still open."

He turned his mount and cantered off along the
street. There was a quiet churchyard at the end of
it, with a kind of square in front of the church
door. In the middle of the square there was a heavy
stone with an anvil on it, and a fine new sword was
stuck through the anvil.

"Well," said the Wart, "I suppose it is some sort
of war memorial, but it will have to do. I am sure
nobody would grudge Kay a war memorial, if they
knew his desperate straits."

He tied his reins round a post of the lych-gate,
strode up the gravel path, and took hold of the
sword.

"Come, sword," he said. "I must cry your mercy
and take you for a better cause."

"This is extraordinary," said the Wart. "I feel
strange when I have hold of this sword, and I notice everything much more clearly. Look at the
beautiful gargoyles of the church, and of the
monastery which it belongs to. See how splendidly
all the famous banners in the aisle are waving. How
nobly that yew holds up the red flakes of its tim-
bers to worship God. How clean the snow is. I can
smell something like fetherfew and sweet briar—
and is it music that I hear?"

It was music, whether of pan-pipes or of recorders, and the light in the churchyard was so clear, without being dazzling, that one could have picked a pin out twenty yards away.

"There is something in this place" said the Wart. "There are people. Oh, people, what do you want?"

Nobody answered him, but the music was loud and the light beautiful.

"People," cried the Wart, "I must take this sword. It is not for me, but for Kay. I will bring it back."

There was still no answer, and Wart turned back to the anvil. He saw the golden letters, which he did not read, and the jewels on the pommel, flashing in the lovely light.

"Come, sword," said the Wart.

He took hold of the handles with both hands, and strained against the stone. There was a melodious consort on the recorders, but nothing moved.

The Wart let go of the handles, when they were beginning to bite into the palms of his hands, and stepped back, seeing stars.

"It is well fixed," he said.

He took hold of it again and pulled with all his might. The music played more strongly, and the light all about the churchyard glowed like amethysts; but the sword still stuck.

"Oh, Merlyn," cried the Wart, "help me to get this weapon."

There was a kind of rushing noise, and a long chord played along with it. All round the churchyard there were hundreds of old friends. They rose over the church wall all together, like the Punch and Judy ghosts of remembered days, and there were badgers and nightingales and vulgar crows and hares and wild geese and falcons and fishes and dogs and dainty unicorns and solitary wasps and corkindrills and hedgehogs and griffins and the thousand other animals he had met. They loomed round the church wall, the lovers and helpers of the Wart, and they all spoke solemnly in turn.

Some of them had come from the banners in the church, where they were painted in heraldry, some from the waters and the sky and the fields about—but all, down to the smallest shrew mouse, had come to help on account of love. Wart felt his power grow.

"Put your back into it," said a Luce (or pike) off one of the heraldic banners, "as you once did when I was going to snap you up. Remember that power springs from the nape of the neck."

"What about those forearms," asked a Badger gravely, "that are held together by a chest? Come along, my dear embryo, and find your tool."

A Merlin sitting at the top of the yew tree cried out, "Now then, Captain Wart, what is the first law of the foot? I thought I once heard something about never letting go?"

"Don't work like a stalling woodpecker," urged a Tawny Owl affectionately. "Keep up a steady effort, my duck, and you will have it yet."

A white-front said, "Now, Wart, if you were once able to fly the great North Sea, surely you can co-ordinate a few little wing-muscles here and there? Fold your powers together, with the spirit of your mind, and it will come out like butter. Come along, Homo sapiens, for all we humble friends of yours are waiting here to cheer."

The Wart walked up to the great sword for the third time. He put out his right hand softly and drew it out as gently as from a scabbard.

EVERYTHING, ALL AT ONCE, TOGETHER

A *Tale of Two Hiccups*

So as to give you a more complete notion as to how metaphors sound and can be used, presented in this Part is an example of an anecdotal metaphor and the transcript of a therapeutic fairy-tale. The example of using anecdotal metaphors (A Tale of Two Hiccups) is actually an account written for me by a therapist trainee (Willie Swensen) who had been trained in the use of metaphors. His account is particularly interesting since it shows two different strategies for alleviating the same problem—hiccups. What makes possible Willie's graceful utilization of these two situations is his ability to be sensitive to the needs of the two people he is working with in setting-up for them a context within which they are free to use their own internal resources in making the changes they need to make.

A Tale of Two Hiccups

While engaged in gainful employment as a busperson at a well known restaurant in the area where I live I encountered a gentleman who was at the mercy of a most annoying and fairly common problem—"hiccups." His waiter had just removed his dinner plate and custom-erily asked him if there was anything else that he desired. The gentleman's reply was to ask for more alcohol and then, framed in a clown-ing manner, used a somewhat distressed tone of voice to ask the waiter if the bar could supply him with something to relieve his hiccups. It was to the distressed portion of his message that I responded.

I approached his table and, in a very serious tone of voice, asked the gentleman, "Do you want to get rid of your hiccups?" His reply was that he did. I then asked him if he would be willing to let me tell him a story, during which he was to make pictures inside his head of the things that I spoke of. After skeptical comments were presented on his part he agreed (at the urging of his fellow diners.)

Immediately I pulled up an empty chair from a nearby table to be able to face him almost completely. In a tonality that was similar to the loud and semi-drunken tone that he used with me during his brief display of skepticism I told him that I was going to tell him a story about a leaky faucet that I had once had, and how that faucet came to be repaired. The gentleman, part of him still choosing to display resistance, turned towards his friends and began to babble his continued skepticisms. In response to this I reached over and grabbed his arm (applying slight pressure) as I repeated my statement about the story I was going to tell him. His immediate response was one of attentiveness. This technique was repeated twice more as I began the story and the gentleman would interrupt by talking. That is, I squeezed his arm and reminded him to "make pictures." Each time I did this he switched to a state of attentiveness. When he became sufficiently attentive I switched to another tonality (one I have found useful in storytelling) and adjusted my voice tempo to match the rhythm of his breathing. This was accompanied on my part by an equally rhythmic bobbing of my head.

As for the story, I told him that I had discovered that I had a leaky faucet, and that the leaky faucet *was causing distress.* I described the action of the dripping using the words *drip . . . drip . . . drip,* making sure to insert as covertly as possible a *drip* each time the gentleman came forth with a hiccup. In

By asking "the gentleman" to restate his desire to get rid of his hiccups Willie secures from him a commitment to the therapeutic relationship. Willie then goes on to specify what it is that "the gentleman" must do.

Notice that throughout Willie calibrates his own behavior from that of the gentleman's. In order to be able to attend to (and give) facial responses, Willie makes sure to sit where they can see one another. Willie also attunes himself to the gentleman's tonality. In fact, Willie adopts the gentleman's tonality at first so as to gain his attention and trust (i.e., meet him at his model of the world.)

Instead of overtly "dealing" with the "resistance" Willie by-passes it completely by arresting the gentleman's attention with an unexpected (and, so, irresistable) grabbing of his arm. By adding his remarks about the task, Willie can then use that grab as an anchor for attentiveness in the gentleman.

Willie's use of voice tempo, head movements, and so on fall under the heading of "pacing." This matching of responses acts as a form of bio-feedback for the gentleman and has the effect of altering his consciousness. (see Bandler and Grinder, 1975 for a complete explanation).

addition to verbally describing the condition of the faucet I used many analogue descriptions and gestures (such as reaching out to turn it off.) As the story progressed I related to him that I finally decided to *call someone who could help me* and that *I called a plumber to fix the leaky faucet.* I told of how I *waited* for the plumber to come and *fix the faucet.* The plumber arrived to *fix the faucet* and he had a bag of tools. I told the plumber about the faucet and he said he could fix it. I said to myself *"how is he going to do it?"* The plumber told me to *"watch carefully."*

I then described both verbally and analogically the taking-apart of the faucet with a rather large wrench the plumber had produced from his bag of tools. I said that the plumber had dismantled the faucet into five pieces. As I gave this description I again inserted a wondering "how is he going to do it?" The plumber told me that the root of the problem was this large red washer. I described the size, thickness, and texture of this washer. The plumber told me to *"look* and *see"* that the washer had a tear in it. Again I asked the plumber if he could repair the faucet and he replied that he could. Again I wondered how he would do it. He said all he needed to do was to replace the washer and the faucet would be fixed. I asked him, *"Do you have a new washer?"* He said that he did. He put in the new washer and put the faucet back together again. I asked him if the faucet was fixed. He said it was. I said I was wondering, "Now, how can I know the faucet is fixed?" He said that there was only one way sure to know and that was to test it. So I turned the water on . . . it came rushing out, and then I turned the handle tightly to turn the water off. And low and behold there was not a drop of water coming from the faucet. The leak had stopped completely.

Throughout the story Willie uses analogue (tonal) marking to mark out important parts for the gentleman (underlined in the narrative.) Also, by having tonally marked *drips* occurring with each hiccup the two are unconsciously connected.

Here quotes are used to have the gentleman ask himself a question ("how"), and to imbed the command that he "watch (i.e., in his head) carefully."

Not only had the leak ceased to be a problem, but so had the gentleman's hiccups. I asked him if he still had the hiccups. To his amazement he discovered that he did not. I immediately rose and left to resume my duties, declining to answer any of his questions. However I did note that his facial expression and tonality had changed markedly (he was much more relaxed.) And when he was leaving the restaurant I informed him that in the future if hiccups should burden him again that he need only squeeze his arm and think of my leaky faucet to gain relief.

What I had done was to create a metaphor for this gentleman's problem—"hiccups." This was accomplished by designing the metaphor to match as closely as possible his internal experience and at the same time allow the story to be general enough so that he might fit his particular internal experience to the patterns presented in the metaphor in the way which was most accurate and comfortable for him. In other words, a metaphor presumes multiple-level communication. At the very least there is the content of the message and there is the context of the message. Obviously the content of the gentleman's problem and the content of the metaphor were distinctly different: one involved hiccups and the other a leaky faucet. Yet the contexts were quite similar. Both involved a man with a problem that caused him great distress. Both contained a person who came to the aid of the man with the problem, and that person made positive statements about being able to help. A reasonable guess would be that he must have been wondering about how I was going to accomplish this. The character in my metaphor also wondered how his faucet would be repaired by the repairman. Also, as I told my tale the gentleman would hiccup from time to time, and for each hiccup I would insert

a head gesture or a *drip*—both, though, were
not so obvious as to cause resistance on his
part. At first I addressed him in his own drunk-
en tone of voice, then later I changed my
tonality and varied it as I wished to mark out
certain portions of my story as separate mes-
sages for him to process. This was further enhanced by analogue gestures and by adjusting
the tempo of my voice to match his breathing.

The purpose of these strategies was to make
my story closely agree with his patterns of
experience on an unconscious level so that
at some point the story I told him would
reach the limits of his model (where he was
"stuck") and with that same patterning allow
him to follow the resolution which was presented in the story. Of course he would at some
level of experience supply his own particular
resolution. As for the elaborate descriptions
that I went through using both verbal and
nonverbal communications to paint him a picture of the problem in the metaphor, that was
primarily for the distraction of his conscious
mind. And, finally, I anchored his experience with me by squeezing his arm, since that
was part of the input throughout the experience. He could then use that anchor to assist
himself in recreating a similar experience in
the future.

*   *   *   *

The strategy of using metaphor as a vehicle of change is to
match as closely as possible the context of internal experience of
the person wishing to make the change. The previous metaphor
example depended largely upon my ability to construct as many
one-to-one correspondences between my story and the person's
problem on the level of context (rather than "content"). However it is my belief that the person's willingness to participate
at the unconscious level determines the ultimate success or failure

of the metaphor in effecting change. In the next example it is necessary for the person to believe that *she* has determined the context for change in order for the metaphor to work. What takes place, then, is the construction of a metaphorical context that satisfies this need.

Again, as before, there was a party of diners at the restaurant where I worked. This time the person with the hiccups was a woman. She commented on her prediciment to the waiter. The waiter, knowing something of my skills, informed her that I could "make her hiccups disappear," and summoned me to do so. I asked her if she would be willing to paint pictures in her head while I told her the story of the leaky faucet. Her response was different from that made by the previous individual with whom I had achieved satisfactory conscious and unconscious agreement as to my intervention in the matter. While responding affirmatively in words to my question, she used a very doubtful tonality and immediately turned away from me to light-up a cigarette. I understood her response to signify that at least part of her was unwilling to have me help her and that that part had certain stakes or investments in defeating what I was going to do. Once again I told my story, but this time results were negative. The woman reported in a somewhat triumphant voice that her hiccups were still with her (which they were). At that point in time a metaphor was constructed that took into account the part of her that needed (for whatever reason) to defeat my efforts. In so doing the context was redefined in favor of solving the problem rather than getting bogged down at the level of a power game. My choice was to tell her that we both knew all along that my story would not help her and to admit my frustration after having taken my best

Perhaps the most important point to be made about this second example is that it is Willie's *willingness to be flexible* in his responses to the situation that allows him to so successfully function as a people-helper.

shot. By this way I was able to accomplish two things. One, I was able to give her resistant part what it wanted (my "defeat" and "control") and, two, since that part had stakes in resisting me it could continue to resist the statements that I was now making to her about how we both knew that the story would not work (therefore, since it did resist—in the form of her arguing—she *had* made an honest effort to cooperate). At this point I left her table so as to allow an even further alliance to form between the part of her that wanted to get rid of her hiccups and the part that was now resisting me by making an honest effort to cooperate to get rid of her hiccups. I returned shortly and asked her the question, "Since my story failed, what color are your hiccups?" To this she replied that they were "purple." I said in a questioning tone of voice, "Your hiccups are purple?", and I walked away. Again I returned very shortly and asked her if she had ever had a purple balloon filled with helium and what happens to a balloon filled with helium when you let go of it? I left immediately. When I returned about three minutes later a very surprised woman told me that she thought that her hiccups were gone. . . and indeed they were.

In this case I allowed her the control of constructing her own metaphor for her hiccups in the form of the color "purple." The next step was merely to connect that with something else that was purple and could serve as a metaphorical means of removing her hiccups. My guess was that she had a reference for what happens when a helium balloon is released. At that point we were no longer talking about hiccups or getting rid of them. We were talking about what happens when one releases a helium balloon. It just so happens that this ballon is purple, and coincidentaly, so are her hiccups.

By simply agreeing with the woman's "resistant part" Willie easily places her in a double bind which requires that she cooperate with him. That is, in order to defeat Willie now she must make the hiccups go away.

Willie here utilizes a synaesthesia cross-over. In this way he can free them both from the volatile issue of her hiccups and instead talk about "purple."

By remaining only long enough to make his interventions (ie. initiate transderivational searches) Willie avoids giving her the opportunity to argue and become tangential.

Willie completes his metaphor with a sub-modality shift, using the balloon as a vehicle.

Vivace's Metaphor

This is the transcript of a metaphor which was told to a young woman (whom we shall call "Vivace") seeking help in improving her eyesight. In the course of the initial interview it was learned that her impaired vision was at least partly due to an *image* she had of her responsibility to take care of her daughter and to not give her father cause to be ashamed of her (Vivace's father was an immigrant from Europe who had some relatively conservative ideas about proper behavior for women). This part of Vivace that focused on her responsibilities was at odds with another part of her that *felt* the need to get away, to dance and move. In the relationship between these two parts of Vivace, the "responsibility" part placated, and the "get away" part blamed.

This metaphor served several therapeutic functions at once. One of its functions was to suggest to Vivace a means by which her conflicting parts can both be satisfied (that is, get what they want for her). A second function was to suggest a way in which Vivace herself can more usefully deal with, and view the behavior of, her father. The third function was to set the tone for subsequent therapy by metaphorically describing the process through which she is likely to go. And, fourth, to suggest to her new ways of using her eyes. In order to accomplish all of these functions, extensive use was made of "stacked realities" in the metaphor.

The First Function

Vivace's "responsibility" part wanted to make sure that she competently cared for her family. That part, however, wasn't really getting what it wanted because Vivace's resentment at being tied to her family sometimes got in the way of her sincere and effective ministering to their needs. Vivace's "get away" part wanted to make sure that she took care of her own needs for relaxation and recreation. This part also missed out on getting what it wanted because Vivace's time to herself was often punctuated with thoughts of responsibilities waiting at home. In the metaphor, the differences between these two parts is clearly delineated. The resolution of their conflict comes when each learns to *level* with the other, both use the *auditory system* with which to communicate with one another, and they learn to share information from each of their representational systems by using *synesthesia patterns*. The consequence of these connecting strategies is that the two parts are now able to communicate effectively, and they are able to use and enhance one another. The patterns look like this:

PROBLEM	CONNECTING STRATEGY	DESIRED OUTCOME
The conflict between two parts is preventing both from being fulfilled	Conflicting parts change the nature of their communications	Both parts (and Vivace) are able to get what they want

OR
(in the metaphor . . .)

PROBLEM	CONNECTING STRATEGY	DESIRED OUTCOME
Let and Ho are trying to be loving sisters, take care of father, and find a path into the garden	They become dependent upon one another in order to achieve their goals	Both Let and Ho achieve their goals and continue to grow as a result

RESOLUTION

METAPHOR	Connecting Strategy	Outcome
Let: $\frac{\text{blamer}}{\text{kinesthetic}}$ →	$\frac{\text{leveler}}{\text{auditory}}$ + synesthesia patterns →	$\frac{\text{leveler}}{}$ kinesthetic auditory visual
Ho: $\frac{\text{placater}}{\text{visual}}$ →	$\frac{\text{leveler}}{\text{auditory}}$ + synesthesia patterns →	$\frac{\text{leveler}}{}$ visual auditory kinesthetic

The Second Function

At one point in the metaphor, Let and Ho's father becomes "blind," and so, from that point on, is unable to "see" the changes in his daughters. Finally, father *asks* to be taken to their "orchard." This trip is accompanied by much talking—the suggestion being that changes in Vivace's father might be best precipitated through his auditory system. Once there, father (a naturally inquisitive man) strikes out on his own. In the story, father's blindness is *not* associated with an intention upon his part to infringe upon the freedom of Let and Ho, but instead is treated as merely an occurrence with which they all deal as best they can.

The Third Function

The entire story line of the metaphor is a description of Vivace's past up until she came to me for help, of the therapeutic relationship, and of some of the changes she can expect to make. Thus, in the story, Let and Ho start out very consonant in their preferences and abilities, diverging only after father becomes "blind." The young man who appears and stays to help with doing "needed chores and repairs" is the therapist (and, on another level, the part of Vivace which has the ability to contact and communicate with her other parts). After Let and Ho have been introduced by the young man to the garden, he leaves since he is no longer necessary. The girls continue to use the orchard as they wish. And in this way the stage is set. Also, it is within the context of the story line that specific anchors are set up by me which are intended to be used at a later date when they can be appropriately used to initiate changes (Let's "wink" and Ho's "pinch on the cheek"). (In fact, including the anchors just mentioned, this metaphor has stacked within it at least seven realities.)

The Fourth Function

The "new ways of using her eyes" include suggestions to *intentionally* use her eye muscles and scanning patterns, to begin to notice the sub-modal aspects of visual information, and to begin to get more information out of what she sees by using synesthesia patterns.

Vivace's Metaphor

In a place not unlike this place, there lived a man and his two daughters. He was a very intelligent man who took great pride in his daughters and provided for them as best he could. They lived in a small house in the forest.

> Notice that it is not specified as to *how* this place is "not unlike" that place, or even what place specifically "this place" is.
>
> "Provided" is left unspecified (provided what?).

His two daughters were named Let and Ho. As youngsters, Let and Ho shared all of their adventures. Each day they would rush out to the forest to make their discoveries. They made little people out of pine cones, and play houses with trees for walls and a sky for a roof. Of course they also saw, and regularly conversed with, all manner of elves, leprachauns, and fairies. And when they were hungry, it didn't take them long to hunt up a bush full of their favorite berries. When they were ready, they would return home, run up to Father and hug him tightly. He hugged them back, laughed, and sat them down on his knee, ready to listen to the particulars of their day's wanderings. He was always fascinated by their adventures, for although he was scholarly, in many ways he was not in touch with the world. He rarely roamed from home, and often wondered what it was like out in the forest.

> Initially, Let and Ho are not only sharing similar needs and expressions of those needs, but both also evidence full development in all of the representational systems.
>
> Notice that such words as "adventures" and "discoveries" are used to cue Vivace that that is what she is doing *now*.
>
> Also, it is not specified as to what way father "was not in touch with the world," thereby providing Vivace with the freedom to fill in what, for her, those "ways" are.

And so it went, year after year. Let and Ho grew together, dropping off worn-out games and replacing them with new ones.

Then one day Father fell unforeseeably and unaccountably blind. Over the time that followed, Let and Ho also began to change. Let continued to spend most of her day romping in the forest. She loved to feel the cool air on her face as she ran, the low branches stinging her legs. She never tired of stroking the furry tufts of green pine needles, or

> Father's falling "unforseeably and unaccountably blind" coincides with Vivace's experience of her father's conservatism, since she was unable to "see why" he should think the way he did.

running her hands over the rough bark of the trees. When she would come upon a berry bush, Let would sometimes take a handful and crush them just because it was such an interesting sensation. And when she was tired, she would lay down on a mossy hillside or on a springy carpet of pine needles.

Ho, on the other hand, saw her place as being in the home. She loved the forest no less than before, and enjoyed gazing at it from the house. She particularly appreciated the blending of colors and shadows as they changed through the day and year. She knew, however, that her greatest pleasure came when she was focusing her attention on the household and its needs. She loved to cook. There was always something special for her about watching a bunch of ingredients combine, disappear into the oven, and emerge obviously changed. Ho also had a talent for seeing what had to be done around the house, and so it was always a picture of orderliness. And, of course, she assumed most of the responsibility for watching out for Father.

Time went on. Often Ho and Let had little to do with one another. And in some ways they got along, and in some ways they didn't. Let would sometimes say to Ho, "You shouldn't spend so much time at home. Why can't you drop that stuff for awhile? And besides, you shouldn't be tending Father so much. He can take care of himself, you know."

Ho would then, reply, "I just know Father needs someone there to watch over him. And I don't mind, really. I like what I do her, and if only you didn't worry about me then everything would be perfect." Even so, once in awhile, Ho would feel stirring within her the need to fly into the forest. But since her duties were clearly at home, she would dim those stirrings as best she could.

It is at this point that Vivace develops two truly distinct parts. Let, the "get away" part, is characterized as being highly kinesthetic here using predicates such as "feel," "cool," "stinging," and so on.

Here Ho, the "responsibility" part, is characterized as being highly visual, using predicates such as "saw," "gazing," "focusing," and so on.

This paragraph brings out the fact that Let and Ho are no longer always consonant with one another.

Let's use of such words as "you shouldn't" and "you can't" indicates her blamer communication mode.

Ho indicates her communication mode of placater here when she uses such words as "just," "if only," and "would."

One day a young man stepped out of the forest and up to the house. Ho saw him first and invited him in. He explained that he was on a journey which, as far as he knew, would never end. And, although Let often pressed him for information, he was quite secretive in many ways. Father, Let, and Ho understood his position, and asked no further questions about his past. The young man asked to stay for awhile in exchange for doing needed chores and repairs. They all agreed.

The narrative goes from indicating that Ho sometimes "felt stirring within her the need to fly into the forest" to the appearance of the young man, who is the therapist.

Not long after the young man had arrived, he came bounding out of the forest calling for Ho. She saw that he was out of breath, and asked him what was the matter.

"Not long" is intentionally not specified.

Notice that Ho is auditorily "called" for.

"Ah," he said, "Ho, I need your help for something that is quite important to us all. Will you see your way clear to join me?"

"Something" is intentionally not specified here.

Ho agreed, and together they set off through the forest. Along the way he said, "We will also need the help of Let. Let's call her."

Using her loudest voice, Ho joined the young man in calling out Let's name. Soon they heard a crashing of underbrush, which was soon followed by Let, picking her way through the bushes. She joined them in their search.

Again, notice that Let is auditorily called for. Also notice the increased use of auditory predicates.

After going a ways, the young man stopped them, and said, "We are here."

"Going a ways" is intentionally not specified, as is "here."

They were standing a short distance away from the edge of a large ravine. The bottom of the ravine was thickly forested. The forest from which they had just emerged ended a number of feet from the edge of the ravine, creating a barren strip of ground that completely ringed the perimeter of the ravine.

"But where *are* we?" both Let and Ho chimed in together.

Let and Ho are now "chiming."

The young man looked wistful and said, "Well, I will tell you. When I was somewhat younger, I met a man on the road. We struck-up

This story-within-a-story told by the young man is

a conversation and decided to travel together for awhile. At one point he removed his hat just long enough for me to get a glimpse of his ears. They were a strange color! When I asked him about his ears, he confessed that he was a sorcerer. After a moment of confusion, I asked him, 'Now that I know that you're a sorcerer, does that mean you won't travel further with me?' It turned out that he was afraid I wouldn't want to stay with *him!* He was very relieved, so we journeyed together until our crossroads. As a parting gift, he told me about a special orchard that produced all manner of strange and delicious fruits. He explained that it was not possible to describe where it was to be found, but did tell me how I would know *when* I had found it."

"How?" both girls whispered.

"A special feeling . . . and I know it's around here."

The three of them then began to search all over for the orchard. Let soon tired and sat down to unknot her hair. Meanwhile, Ho continued to scan, looking for a sign. She walked carefully to the edge of the ravine . . . and peered intently at its forested floor.

Then she saw it.

Down in the trees, through a small opening in the leaves, she saw the sunlight reflected off of a colored surface. As she looked closer, she could see by the way in which the light played upon that surface that it was smooth, curved to make a sphere, and it was hard . . . and definitely worth going after. Now she also noticed that it was a very warm, deep red. She felt tingly inside as she watched a beam of light fall there.

"There it is," she said in a calm voice as she pointed into the ravine. Let and the young man followed her pointing finger until they too saw it.

actually another metaphor for the therapeutic relationship between Vivace and the therapist. This substory is also used as a means of suggesting to Vivace that she can use her feelings to tell her when something is "right" for her.

Ho's highly developed visual system is here framed as useful—that is, she is able to locate the orchard. Notice, however, that her recognizing the orchard is tied in with making significant cross-overs between visual and kinesthetic submodalities (e.g., by the light "playing" on the surface she could see that it was "smooth," "curved," and "hard;" it is "red" and, so, "warm").

"You've found it," he whispered, and he gently pinched her right cheek. "Now, how will we reach it?" All three stood on the brink of the ravine and looked down at the steep walls which appeared to surround it. Ho spent some time looking over the steep walls, checking for a path or entrance. But she soon got eyestrain, and so she sat down on the ledge and dangled her feet.

Finally, Let knew what she had to do. "I'll get down there," she intoned. With that, she lowered herself over the edge. She felt carefully with her feet for whatever footholds she could find. At the same time she grasped with her hands what secure stones or roots were within reach. She made her way down a few feet, then ran out of places to place her feet. She slipped a few times. It was then that she looked down at her feet. As she gazed at the area around them, she noticed that by looking for the shadows she could clearly identify likely crevices and footholds. Consequently, she was able to continue with considerable ease. At one point, she called up to the others waiting at the ledge:

"Watch me closely," she yelled, "and it will be easy for you to follow!" It was then that the young man winked at her with his left eye.

He and Ho carefully watched all of the graceful movements that Let used, and soon they too were nimbly climbing down into the ravine.

In the ravine, they scattered about, chattering like a flock of birds. Then they came upon the special orchard. And it was indeed special. All manner of strange trees and bushes grew there. And from each there was hanging myriads of exotically shaped and colored fruits. Some even changed shape or color as they were handled. Each had a special texture to its skin. Some went from being rough to being smooth

The pinch that Ho receives here was analogue marked by voice tonality so that it could be used as an anchor for Vivace using both her visual and kinesthetic systems to "find things."

Let's highly developed kinesthetic system is reframed here as being useful—that is, she is able to make a path to the orchard.

As with Ho before, Let's success is made contingent upon her ability to use her kinesthetic system in conjunction with her visual system.

Let's experience of discerning a "path" is also anchored for subsequent use by means of tonally marking the "winking" sentence.

The descriptions of the various "fruits" in the orchard are all intentionally unspecified, providing Vivace with the maximum opportunity to make of those fruits what she will.

Notice the extensive use of synesthesia patterns used

when gently squeezed. There were dense ones and fluffy ones, both large and small. When you shook this one, it rattled. When you plucked that one, it "popped." And still another made the most pleasant crackling sound when it was opened. All day they spent in tasting and experimenting with the fruits. Many were delightfully delicious and satisfying. Some were quite bitter, but they rapidly discovered that the bitter ones had many other uses. A most remarkable orchard.

here in describing the fruits, and the use of submodalities in general.

"Bitter fruits" are reframed as being "useful."

Each day they would return to the orchard. And each time they descended or ascended the ravine wall, they would make their trail a little more worn, until they were soon walking a pleasant path to their special place. Once in the orchard, they would enjoy wonderful conversations in which they discovered much about one another. Ho found that her walks into the forest were so relaxing and invigorating that taking care of the house became easier and more enjoyable. And Let soon began to see ways in which she could bring the things she had learned about the forest into their home, and in that way became a vital part of them both.

The orchard is described as a place which is easier to get to each time, and as a place of "conversations" leading to "discoveries."

Also reframed here is the ability of all of the representational systems to enhance both Let and Ho.

One day Ho and Let awoke to discover that the young man had gone. They didn't fret, for they had always known that he would someday leave . . . . They had always known that the orchard they had found wasn't his orchard.

And so, together, Let and Ho continued their trips of comfort and discovery to their orchard.

One morning Father said, "Well, it's long overdue, but certainly not too late. Daughters, be so kind as to show me the way to that orchard." Ho took him by the right hand, and Let took him by the left. Together they led him through the forest, all of them talking gaily as they went. When they reached the ravine,

Father said, "Let me go for a moment . . .
there is something I must find out for myself."

Father then took small steps toward the
brink of the ravine. When he reached the edge
he dangled one of his feet over into the emptiness, and smiled.

"I always wondered," he said. "If you ladies
will take my hands now, I'm ready to visit
this orchard of yours."

They led him down the path. When they
reached the bottom, Father spoke again,
"Leave me be now. I'll find it on my own . . ."
Let and Ho were worried about him at first,
but after talking it over they decided that it
was important. So while they sat in the orchard, Father meandered about the ravine
floor. Sometimes he smacked up against a tree.
Sometimes he tripped and fell. Let and Ho
always knew where he was, because they could
hear him giggling to, and about, himself.

Father at last *did* find the orchard, and he
spent the afternoon wandering from plant to
plant, tasting whatever he could. Let and Ho
felt very pleased and so at ease that they soon
forgot about Father (who was, at that point,
not in the least interested in being remembered). Instead, Let and Ho continued to dream
their dreams and discuss their hopes.

And so it went. They returned to the little
orchard whenever they needed to and whenever
they wanted to. And sometimes that was
often. And sometimes it was not. But they
always knew that it was

there . . .

ENVOY

"I was returning from high school one day and a runaway horse with a bridle on sped past a group of us into a farmer's yard . . . looking for a drink of water. The horse was perspiring heavily. And the farmer didn't recognize it, so we cornered it. I hopped on the horse's back . . . since it had a bridle on, I took hold of the rein and said, 'Giddy-up' . . . headed for the highway. I knew the horse would turn in the right direction . . . I didn't know what the right direction was. And the horse trotted and galloped along. Now and then he would forget he was on the highway and start into a field. So I would pull on him a bit and call his attention to the fact the highway was where he was supposed to be. And finally about four miles from where I had boarded him he turned into a farm yard and the farmer said, 'So that's how that critter came back. Where did you find him?'

"I said, 'About four miles from here.'

"'How did you know he should come here?'

"I said, 'I didn't know . . . the horse knew. All I did was keep his attention on the road.'

". . . . . . . I think that's the way you do psychotherapy."

Milton H. Erickson, M.D.
Phoenix, Arizona
March 21, 1978

BIBLIOGRAPHY

BIBLIOGRAPHY

Bach-y-Rita, Paul. *Brain Mechanisms in Sensory Substitution*. New York: Academic Press, 1972.

Bandler, Richard, and Grinder, John. *The Structure of Magic, Vol. I*. Palo Alto, California: Science and Behavior Books, 1975.

Bandler, Richard, and Grinder, John. *Patterns of the Hypnotic Techniques of Milton H. Erickson, M.D., Vol. I*. Cupertino, California: Meta Publications, 1975.

Bandler, Richard; Grinder, John; and Satir, V. *Changing With Families*. Palo Alto, California: Science and Behavior Books, 1976.

Bettelheim, Bruno. *The Uses of Enchantment*. New York: Alfred Knopf, 1975.

Campbell, Joseph. *The Hero with a Thousand Faces*. New York: Pantheon Books, 1949.

Fromm, Erich. *The Forgotten Language; An Introduction to the Understanding of Dreams, Fairytales, and Myths*. New York: Rinehart & Co., 1951.

Grinder, John, and Bandler, Richard. *The Structure of Magic, Vol. II*. Palo Alto, California: Science and Behavior Books, 1976.

Grinder, John; DeLozier, Judith; and Bandler, Richard. *Patterns of the Hypnotic Techniques of Milton H. Erickson, M.D., Vol. II*. Cupertino, California: Meta Publications, 1977.

Haley, Jay (ed.). *Advanced Techniques of Hypnosis and Therapy*. New York: Grune and Stratton, 1967.

Haley, Jay. *Uncommon Therapy: The Psychiatric Techniques of Milton H. Erickson*. New York: W. W. Norton & Co., 1973.

Kopp, Sheldon. *Guru: Metaphors from a Psychotherapist.* Palo Alto, California: Science and Behavior Books, 1971.

Miller, G. A. "The magical number seven, plus or minus two: Some limits on our capacity for processing information." *Psychological Review* 63 (1956):81-97.

Miller, G. A.; Galanter, E.; and Pribram, K. *Plans and the Structure of Behavior.* New York: Holt, Rinehart, and Winston, Inc., 1960.

Pribram, Karl. *Languages of the Brain.* Englewood Cliffs, New Jersey: Prentice-Hall, Inc., 1971.

Satir, Virginia. *Peoplemaking.* Palo Alto, California: Science and Behavior Books, 1972.

Turbayne, Collin. *The Myth of Metaphor.* London: Yale University Press, 1962.

APPENDIX:
Research into Sub-Modalities

RESEARCH INTO SUB-MODALITIES

This appendix represents a condensation of the preliminary re-
search I have done on sub-modalities and, so, is not to be taken as
an exhaustive presentation of the subject. It is, instead, being
offered with the hope that this particular reorganization of what
we already know will excite others to further explore the pro-
found implications and consequences of sub-modality patterns
within the contexts of psychology, neurophysiology, neuro-
anatomy, communications theory, and related fields. As will
become clear in the pages to follow, this approach makes possible
a useful reevaluation of the significance of past behavioral, per-
ceptual, and neurophysiological research and points the way to
new ways of organizing future research. The field is wide open.

Representation

One of the primary functions of psychology and psychological
research is to illuminate the relationship between the objective
world and the world of experience. The medium through which
the objective (palpable) world is experienced is that of sensory
experience (that is; vision, audition, kinesthesis, olfaction, and
taste).

As fellow human beings, we are each endowed with essentially
equivalent sensory apparatuses. The eyes, middle and inner ears,
Pacinian corpuscles, olfactory bulbs, and taste buds belonging to
any two individuals are anatomically and physiologically identical
for all practical purposes. As more and more neurophysiological
and correlative behavior evidence is amassed, it is also becoming
evident that the sub-cortical and cortical neural pathways and

projection areas which serve those sensory mechanisms are also very characteristic of human brains in general.

Despite this use of similar "equipment," it is also evident that no two individuals using that "equipment" will perceive a particular occurrence in the world in exactly the same way. The difference that exists between individuals in their perceptions of their environment can be explained on both the level of *selective attention to input (sensory) channels*, and on the level of *variations of experience with sensory inputs*.

By "selective attention to input (sensory) channels," we are referring to the phenomenon that at any moment in time an individual *usually* attends to (is conscious of) one, or possibly two, of his sensory systems. Since consciousness is limited to approximately 7 ± 2 "chunks" of information at any moment, the ability to selectively attend to a sensory channel can, at times, become necessary or advantageous when the information coming through a particular channel is important or critical. By selectively attending to such a sensory channel, we are able to consciously glean as much information from it as we can at that moment. Meanwhile, information contained in the other sensory systems which is less relevant can be ignored. We have all had the experience of being intently involved in a conversation (auditory) only to eventually discover that an acquaintance has been standing alongside for some time (visual). Or perhaps you have had the experience of reading a fascinating book, discovering *later* that someone had announced that your dinner was waiting. If not for this ability to focus attention, we would have in consciousness much irrelevant information, and would have to depend to a much greater extent upon redundance in our environment in order to amass relevant discriminations.

As indicated in the examples above, the selection of a particular sensory modality as a focus for attention is often determined by the kind of information an individual is seeking. For example, our intent conversationalist above "needed" to depend upon his auditory system for most of the relevant information in that particular situation. If we now make the third person (who "miraculously" appears) an artist looking for faces to sketch, he will no doubt disregard the text of the conversation in favor of attending to the visible facial features of the other two. Such "attentions" are not, then, *neurologically patterned*, but are the contextually dependent result of individual intention and the environment.

Selective attention is not always *ad hoc*, however. As already discussed in Part IV on representational systems, each individual learns to depend upon one sensory system or another as a means of perceiving and understanding the world. This dependence upon particular representational systems is characteristic of human beings in general, and generates patterns of experience among individuals and within an individual. These patterns have already been discussed in Parts IV, V, and VI (further specification of these patterns can be found in Grinder and Bandler, 1976; and in Bandler and Grinder, 1975).

So, one reason that we each have different experiences of the same environment is that we intentionally or characteristically attend to different aspects of that environment. It is something like a cooking class. Since each of us selects some similar and some different ingredients in similar and varying proportions, we each end up with something different to put into the oven.

Meaning

Differentiation of experience does not stop there, however. In order to be of use perceptual experiences must be *meaningful*. That is, a perceptual experience must convey some useful information about the environment. Neuronal firing (even patterned neural activity) does not convey any information about the environment—only about the activity of the sensory end-organ with which it is connected. What makes that pattern of neural firing meaningful is the individual's previous experience with that firing pattern. What makes a particular perception meaningful, then, is our previous experiences with that perception. For example, the word MAD is easily recognizable by most English-speaking people as a meaningful configuration of letters. On the other hand, the similar configuration of letters MDA is just as easily recognized as meaning*less*. The point is that before one is taught lexical English, the configuration MAD is no more or less meaningful than the configuration MDA. The way in which meaningfulness is developed is by the *correlation of perceptual experiences*. As soon as a fetus is capable of storing information it is capable of meaningfully perceiving its environment in a way which can be illustrated as follows:

Until a child has touched or come close to it, a candle flame is neither hot nor cold. All that is apparent is that it is of a certain color and shape. Once the flame has been touched, however, that color and shape become meaningful indicators of a correlative experience—"pain" and/or "hot." Later, when that child hears the word "flame," it is a meaningless set of sounds until he or she is shown, at the same time, a flame. When in school the child is presented with another meaningless experience—the configuration of letters FLAME. Once those letters are paired with a picture of a flame, or the spoken word, they too become meaningful (that is, correlated with previous experiences). Beyond the illustration of correlative learning, there are two important points to be noticed about our fiery example:

The first is that in some instances the correlation of perceptual experiences occurs *between* two or more different sensory modalities, and in others correlation occurs *intra*-modally. In the first part of the example, the child correlates a visual perception with a kinesthetic one. In the second part, the child correlates an auditory perception with a visual (and perhaps the "memory" of a kinesthetic) perception. And, in the third part, a visual perception is correlated with another visual and/or auditory perception. Therefore, *"an experience" is built up through the correlation of perceptual discriminations within and between various sensory modalities.*

The second point to be noticed is that each of the perceptual discriminations the child makes is described by only certain aspects of each of the modalities used. That is, the discrimination did not occur on the modality level, but on the *sub-modality* level. When we "see" we determine what it is we are viewing in terms of the object's visually qualitative dimensions. We determine its color, size, shape, brightness, location, and so on. These "qualitative dimensions" are the *sub-modalities* for vision. ("Sub-modalities" are more fully discussed in Part V.) In our example, upon first contact the child correlated his sub-modality discriminations of the candle flame's appearance with his sub-modality discriminations of the kinesthetic sensations of hot/pain. One correlation that could come out of this experience is "red-hot." As the child grew and made more correlations, he probably learned that certain visual configurations of color, brightness, shape, and movement signified "hot," so that he would not be afraid to touch an apple.

The question then becomes: are correlations between and within sub-modalities (such as "red-hot") basic operating premises in perception which are then summed with other contextual information to produce "an experience," or are experiences stored as contextual information to be triggered by matching sensory information?

These experiences/perceptions/correlations/configurations of sub-modalities are stored holographically within the brain to be later used as material for subsequent correlations (see Pribram, 1971, for a lucid argument favoring holographic storage). Thus, once you have stored the experience "picture-of-flame"—"flame," subsequently hearing the word "flame" is a meaningful experience *because* it evokes a correlative experience (i.e., an image of a flame). Most correlative experiences are contextually dependent, and so are arbitrary (for instance, the assignation of words to "stand for" various objects and events). Some correlative experiences, however, seem so pervasive and consistent among individuals that they seem to function more as basic premises for experience than as contextually (arbitrarily) derived correlations.

For example, "red" is considered by most people to be a "warm" color regardless of whether it is the red of a flame, an apple skin, or a drapery. An example of a context dependent correlation would be the shape. $\lozenge$ If you are told that that shape is a "candle flame," it becomes correlated with "hot;" but if you are told that it is a "water drop," it becomes correlated with "cool." This means that in encountering an environmental event with which one has no previous experience, one will be able to use only the *premise* correlations as a means of making meaning out of it, since contextually dependent correlations are fixed and narrow in range. Thus, MAD is meaningful and MDA is not meaningful because such configurations of letters are arbitrary and context-specific, rather than patterned in terms of sensory experience.

Our examples, therefore, indicate that there is a patterned relationship between the sub-modalities of *color* and *temperature*, and that there is as yet no indication of a patterned relationship between *shape* and *temperature*. The purpose of this study is to begin to delineate what is already experimentally known about how sub-modalities interact with one another, and to what extent those interactions are systematic. Since, as discussed in Part V, experience occurs at the sub-modality level, knowing precisely how and to what extent sub-modalities interact will provide researchers and therapists with a systematic and secure foundation upon which an understanding of human experience can be built.

Inter- and Intra-Sensory Interactions

There have been many experiments demonstrating that sub-modalities affect one another in various ways. Research now strongly indicates that sensory, motor, and association areas in the cortex can no longer be considered discreet areas of function (Masterson and Berkley, 1974). Instead, these areas are extensively interconnected, so that (for example) stimulation of an auditory area produces corresponding neural activity in the visual and kinesthetic projection areas (Bach-y-Rita, 1972; Eccles, 1966; Pribram, 1971). Such studies may, perhaps, provide the physiological explanations for the mountain of research which has been done on the fact that sensory systems *do* interact. For example, Mainwaring (1932) showed (unintentionally) that most people recall auditory experiences using a visual or kinesthetic cue of some kind. Also, these inter-modal effects are reciprocal. For instance, Jordan (1968) reports in a study on autokinetic movement that subjects felt their eyes to be "pulled" in a direction opposite to that moved by the light source. Reciprocally, Davies (1973) reports that part and whole body movements qualitatively affect after-images. Intra-modality interactions also occur, as illustrated in an important article by Gellhorn (1964) in which he shows how facial and skeletal muscle position and use affects whole-body feelings.

The question now becomes: to what extent are these patterns of modality interaction characteristic of human beings in general, and to what extent are they characteristic of individuals? Little work has been done on this question. Henion (1970) has found only "some" support for consistency in cross-modality interactions between the visual and olfactory systems. In a simple yet elegant study on personal perceptual styles when observing autokinetic movement, Santos, Farrow, and Haines (1965) found that although there were great inter-individual differences as to observed patterns of movement, each subject showed remarkable personal consistency in movement patterns (see illustration on page 220).

We will look at additional information regarding "perceptual styles" in a later section in this appendix. It can be said now, however, that what little experimental evidence there is, and logic, indicates that some patterns of sub-modal interaction are characteristic of human perceptual strategies (both learned and genetic) and that other patterns are characteristic of individuals. In support of this assertion, let us now look at additional experimental evidence regarding intra- and inter-modality interactions.

Modal Interaction

Many investigators have attempted to determine how the visual and haptic-proprioceptive (kinesthetic) systems affect one another. Most of these studies involve comparisons of intra-modal to inter-modal ability to match visually and/or haptically presented stimuli. In their experiment, Connolly and Jones (1970) found that the most accurate matching of line length is done within the

AUTOKINETIC MOTION: CONSISTENCY AND STYLE

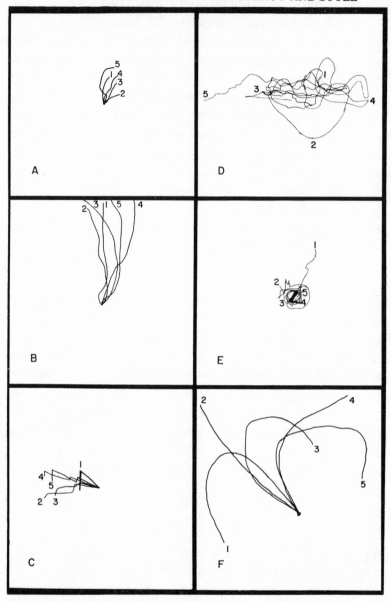

FIG. 1. Samples of *S*s judged as showing high degrees of similarity (Examples A, B, C) and dissimilarity (Examples D, E, F) of experiences on five AK trials

visual system (that is, visual stimuli → visual comparison). They also found that the visual → kinesthetic case was the least accurate, and that the kinesthetic → kinesthetic and kinesthetic → visual cases were about the same in terms of accuracy. In a study by Davidson, Abbott, and Gershenfeld (1974), however, nearly opposite results were found. In their study, they varied the amount of time allowed for visual and/or kinesthetic inspection and so showed that when subjects are given more time to feel the standard and comparison stimuli, kinesthetic → kinesthetic matching is as accurate as visual → visual matching. Also, in their experiment, visual → kinesthetic matching was *more* accurate than kinesthetic → visual discriminations (see also, Appelle, 1971). A third study, by Krauthamer (1959), found that there was *no* difference between the accuracy of kinesthetic → kinesthetic matching and kinesthetic → visual or visual → kinesthetic matching. Obviously, no conclusions can be drawn from these disparate studies other than that they indicate some serious oversights in considering the parameters of the problem.

One source of possible error in the above studies is that which was pointed out by Jones (1973). He demonstrated that when making inter-modality comparisons, one must take into consideration the difference between active kinesthetic exploration (i.e., voluntary movements by the subject) and passive kinesthetic exploration. In his study, active exploration led to errors of underestimation, while passive exploration resulted in overestimation of stimuli.

Another consideration is the one discussed by Miller (1973). Miller found that in visual → kinesthetic matching tasks visual input overrides kinesthetic input when they are in conflict. When not in conflict, kinesthesis is independent of vision. Support for this finding comes from Schiffrin and Grantham (1974) who demonstrated that monitoring *simultaneously* the visual, auditory, and kinesthetic input channels does not reduce the ability to make detections of threshold stimuli. Subject expectation of dealing with a single object (when in fact there were two) also induced visual dominance in Miller's experiments. A study comparing blind-from-birth and sighted subjects of varying ages supports Miller's finding that the visual system will exert a greater degree of bias on the kinesthetic system than vice versa. This same study by Warren and Pick, Jr. (1970) also showed that the kinesthetic systems exerts more influence over auditory discrimination than does the auditory over the kinesthetic (see also Harris, 1965).

(Bear in mind as you evaluate the above and the following findings that, as we saw in Part IV, human beings characteristically represent most of their experiences through one of the primary sensory systems. Since "visuals" are very much over-represented in our culture, they will also be over-represented in subject populations and will consequently bias experimental results. Until now, researchers have not explicitly known about primary representational systems, and so all research into human perception is subject to reevaluation with respect to personal sensory system preferences. Viz . . .)

A variable that is virtually never considered in the research is the possibility that experimental results are due to strategies of information gathering characteristic of each of the subjects. For example, in an inter-intra-modality study by McDonnell and Duffett (1972) using wooden blocks as stimuli, there was found no visual or kinesthetic dominance for the task. What they *did* observe was that some of their subjects reported using primarily visual information in order to make their judgements, while other subjects reported using primarily kinesthetic information. A direct illustration of the point comes from Peterson, Holsten, and Spevak (1975) who published a study in which their subjects were required to "imagine" (i.e., internally picture) patterns of dashes and dots. In describing their results they note that they had to disregard the test results of one subject because that person, for some reason, appeared to be unable to make internal pictures!

A fourth possible source of variation is illustrated by a study done by Abravanel (1971), which also investigated inter-intra-modality line-matching competencies. An analysis of his results shows that the highest number of errors occurs when the modality used to *report* the judgement is the *same* as that used to *make* the judgement. The following chart summarizes the error extremes for Abravanel's two experiments:

REPORT MODALITY

	Exp I		Exp II	
	Visual		Haptic	
Lowest # Errors	H	V	V	V
Highest # Errors	V	V	H	H

A final point to be considered here is that perhaps the stimuli used in these experiments convey different *meaning* in different modalities. Recall now our discussion in the first section regarding the acquisition of meaning. It may be that the stimuli used are meaningful for the subject in terms of one set of past experiences when presented to his visual system, but are meaningful in terms of an overlapping but *different* set of past experiences when presented to the kinesthetic system for judgement. If so, then the subjects of the above-cited studies may not have been examining the "same" stimuli with their eyes as with their hands. In order to specify these differences, we must first specify how modalities interact at the *sub-modal* level, and in what ways do sub-modalities *systematically* affect one another. Once this has been done, we will be truly ready to understand what is occurring in more complex experience (that is, experience involving simultaneous representation in many sub-modalities).

Development of the Modalities

The confusion regarding the interaction of modalities is in no way lessened by looking at the problem from the developmental viewpoint. Blank and Klig (1970) found that, for four-year-olds, kinesthetic → visual learning was as good as visual → visual learning. Similarly, Milne (1969) found transfer of learning in children going from kinesthetic to visual superior to the reverse situation.

Rudel and Teuber (1964) observed that 4-5 year-olds were most effective at making visual → visual discriminations, least effective at kinesthetic → kinesthetic discriminations, with bi-modal discriminations falling in between (see also Butter and Zung, 1970). Finally, a study by Millar (1972) showed visual → kinesthetic judgements of distance to produce the highest number of errors among four-year-olds, and kinesthetic → visual judgements the more error-producing for 6-8 year old children.

Taken together, these studies indicate that for children four to eight years old, visual → visual matching is most effective and kinesthetic → kinesthetic matching is probably least effective. This finding agrees fairly well with those from the adult samples. Also, both Blank and Klig's study and that by Butter and Zung agree that for four-year-olds, kinesthetic → visual discriminations are better than the reverse. This does not, however, agree with some of the findings cited above for adults. But, if Davidson, et al., are correct about the superior accuracy of visual → kinesthetic matching, then that taken with Millar's findings for 6-8 year old children would indicate that there occurs a reversal by age six such that it becomes easier to correlate visual input with kinesthetic output, than to input-output the reverse.

Of interest along the lines of development is Spencer's (1970) study that the intra- and inter-modality matching accuracy of elderly people more closely resembles that of children (age six) than that of young adults. This finding lends support to Millar's conclusion in that it shows that the ability to process information through the various modalities, like many other behavioral and psychophysiological aging phenomena, progressively changes throughout an individual's lifetime, with a tendency towards resuming the functioning level of a child.

The Sub-Modalities

We can now consider some of the specific ways in which sub-modalities affect one another. The studies which are cited in this section are a representative, rather than exhaustive, listing of the research that has directly or incidentally touched on sub-modality relationships. One of the problems with evaluating such research is that much, or most, of it was conducted without an explicit appreciation for the functioning of perception at the sub-modality level.

Frequency

The two sub-modalities most directly suggested by *frequency* are that of "color" in the visual system, and "pitch" in the auditory system. Intra-modaly, "color" has been shown to affect visual judgements of size (Wallis, 1935). In Wallis's study, blocks of wood appeared to be larger or smaller depending upon the color it had been painted. Going from largest-apparent-size to smallest-apparent-size, the subject ranking of colors was yellow, white, red, green, blue, and black. These early findings are corroborated in subsequent research by Bevan and Dukes (1953) and by Sato (1955). Although not specifically tested in his experiments, Wallis found indications that luminosity also affects size discrimination.

Color exerts a similar and stronger effect on judgements of object weight (Payne, 1958; Payne, 1961). Objects which are black, blue, or red, tend to be judged heavier than identical objects which are green, yellow, or white. Payne also considers that luminosity ("reflectance") is a factor in these discriminations. Along these lines, McCain and Karr (1970) found that object color affected distance discrimination, such that red objects appeared to be closer and blue objects further away than they really were.

In his book, Birren (1950) suggests that different colors actually evoke or correspond to different geometric shapes. For example, orange supposedly evokes the image of a rectangle; yellow, a pyramid or inverted triangle; blue, a circle; and red, sharp angles, squares, or cubes.

More apparent is the connection between colors and "moods" or "emotions." Birren cites studies which indicate that in our culture colors are frequently correlated with general emotional/

behavioral states. For instance, red evokes restlessness and aggression, yellow evokes industriousness and jealousy, blue or green evokes calmness and security, and so on. Luscher (Scott, 1969) and his famous color test represents what is most certainly the most detailed analysis of color/emotion correlations.

Spectral frequency has always been intimately tied to our perceptions of temperature. In an early study by Podolsky (1938) it was found that office workers working in a recently-painted blue room complained of the "cold," even though the thermostat had not been touched, and even when it was subsequently raised. These complaints stopped when the room was repainted yellow, and did not resume even when the thermostat was set lower than normal. More recent studies indicate that the degree to which colors are associated with temperatures is a matter of personal preference, and that such associations are culturally determined rather than genetically determined. In a study by Berry (1961), subjects showed no differences in temperature tolerance under different color illuminations, but they persisted in ranking colors in terms of "hot" and "cold." In testing six, twelve, and eighteen year-olds, Morgan, Goodson, and Jones (1975) found that the eighteen-year-olds made the conventional matches of color to temperature, while the only reliable match for the two younger groups was "red-hot." In the opinion of these investigators, such associations are culturally determined.

Even if such associations are learned, however, it is not at all certain that such learning is culturally, rather than physiologically, determined. Both blood pressure and pulse rate initially increase (then drop to normal) in response to the red-violet end of the spectrum, while blue light produces the opposite effect (Birren, 1950). Similarly, Podolsky (1938) cites evidence that breathing rate tends to increase under red light. There is also evidence now for cutaneous discrimination of colors (Nash, 1969). Thus, it may be that our physiology is the basis of the color-temperature synesthesia pattern.

Spectral frequency has also been shown to influence perception of sweetness and acidity (Vicente and Vicente, 1968). Similarly, Holt-Hansen (1968) has reported that auditory frequency also affects taste. In his study, subjects associated different beers with specific pitchs. These matchings were almost identical for each of the subjects, indicating the presence of generally held rules of synesthesia rather than subject-unique rules. From verbatim descriptions made by the subjects, it is also obvious that other modalities were used in correlating taste with tones. One subject, for example, described the taste in terms of its "bitterness, body, and smoothness," while another had an image of being in the shade among "straight and upright beech trees." One subject noted that when the continuously present comparison tone deviated in pitch from that which corresponded with the beer, his ability to taste and smell disappeared (Holt-Hansen, pp. 65-66).

Pitch also affects visual perception in many ways. Following is a summary of these inter-sensory effects as reported in reviews by Ryan (1940) and London (1954).

1. Auditory stimulation affects color perception only when the colors are "unstable, filmy, and low in saturation." Low tones make colors "darker, warmer, 'unclear,' and 'dirty.' With high tones colors usually become brighter, colder, sharply contoured, and more solid or surfacy."

2. Hue is also affected. Low tones produce a shift towards red, blue, or violet; and high tones towards yellow and green. The reverse effect also occurs.

3. Auditory beats affect visual flicker frequency.

4. Average or above average intensity in a sound tends to reduce peripheral vision sensitivity. A period of hyperventilation will restore sensitivity even if noise level continues.

5. Ultrasonic frequencies may increase peripheral sensitivity.

6. Auditory stimulation effects upon visual flicker frequency depend upon the color used: the CFF of a green light will be reduced; and the CFF of a red-orange light increased.

7. Auditory stimulation increases sensitivity of the dark adopted eye to blue-greens; and decreases sensitivity to red-orange.

8. Loud noises impair brightness discrimination.

9. White light increases auditory sensitivity, and no light decreases sensitivity. In a green-illuminated room auditory sensitivity is increased; and in a red-illuminated room sensitivity is reduced.

Intensity

The ability to transmit information regarding the *intensity* of a stimulus is characteristic of all of the five sensory systems. In the visual system, intensity occurs as "brightness," in the auditory system as "loudness," and in the kinesthetic system as "pressure." Intensity in the gustatory and olfactory systems is probably best represented by "concentration."

In the visual system, a dark surround increases the apparent brightness of a color and at the same time reduces that color's apparent saturation (purity) (Pitt and Winter, 1974; see also Lie, 1969). Such a relationship could be easily attributed to lateral inhibition in the retina. Another finding which is probably attributable to neural processing is that as central plane luminance increases, the visual field decreases (Zahn and Haines, 1971). The experience of discomfort due to brightness is apparently not due to the perception of brightness *per se*, but to an intensity-pain mechanism that is separate (and similar to the somaesthetic intensity-pain mechanism) (Bourassa and Wirtschafter, 1966).

Although changing the brightness of a particular color does not alter its apparent hue, different colors reflecting equal "amounts" of light *do* appear to be different in brightness (Gregory, 1966). This differential sensitivity of the retina causes colors occurring in the middle of the spectrum (green and yellow) to *appear* brighter than the colors occurring at either end of the spectrum (purple, blue → orange, red).

The reverse intensity-frequency relationship occurs in the auditory system. The phenomen, as demonstrated by Stevens (1936), was that as intensity increased, the pitch of relatively high-frequency tones increased; and as the intensity decreased, the pitch of relatively low tones decreased.

Loud sounds of about eighty decibels produces a 37% decrease in stomach contractions, so that those contractions closely resemble those occurring during the "fear response" (Smith and Laird, 1930) (Milner, 1970, reports that the range of audition from detection threshold to "pain" is about 120 decibels). Very loud sounds of up to 170 decibels are also capable of producing sensations of "tickle," "warmth," "pain," and "dizziness" (Ades, et al., 1958). More recently, Gescheider (1970) found that, using only intensity as a cue, the skin can localize sound nearly as well as can the auditory system.

Little has been done on the inter-modal effects of kinesthetic pressure. McFarland (1971) found some effect of cutaneous pressure upon magnitude estimations of temperature (such that increased pressure decreased temperature sensitivity), but the results are not conclusive. When Velhagen (1936) placed subjects in a pressure chamber, he found that the increased pressure decreased their ability to discriminate colors and brightness levels.

Purity

Beyond the sub-modal classes of *frequency* and *intensity* the correspondence between sub-modalities becomes more a matter of personal preference than of logical or empirical correlation. Under the sub-modal class of *purity*, I choose to include:

in the *visual* system: "saturation," which is determined by the purity of the hue;

in the *auditory* system: "timber," which is determined by the purity of the wave form;

in the *kinesthetic* system: "texture," which is determined by the pattern of cutaneous deformation; and,

in the *olfactory* system: "essence," which is determined by the purity of the odor's characteristic properties.

Very little research has been directed at evaluating these sub-modalities, and even less has been done to illuminate their inter-modal relationships. In addition to this lack of information (or perhaps because of it) there exists no appropriately defined and adequately descriptive vocabulary capable of handling these and other sub-modality distinctions. One of the primary aims of this monograph is to re-stimulate interest and research into the area of perception—*but perception at the sub-modality level.* Consequently, the classes of sub-modalities which are defined here are intended to act as a point of departure—as a model which is designed to be restructured as you begin to discern the adequacies and inadequacies of its various parts. For example, one issue which is side-stepped in the present treatment of the class *purity* is that of discriminating "texture" visually. Is "texture" a legitimate sub-modality of the visual system, or is it more accurately described as a perception resulting from the correlation of certain sub-modalities? Can the visual perception of "texture" be adequately accounted for by variations in "saturation," or in "brightness?" This is the level at which we must begin. You do not need to know how a house is built in order to live in it—but if you want to know how it is able to hold its roof up, you will have to look at the arrangement of *2 X 4's* within the walls.

About the only consideration that has been given to "saturation" in the experimental literature has been in controlling saturation in color discrimination experiments. One of the few experimental references to saturation has already been cited above under *frequency* (high and low auditory tones can affect the saturation characteristics of a hue). Also, it was mentioned under *intensity* that a dark surround decreases saturation. No data seems to be available on the effect of "saturation" upon perception. One study on visual textures, however, did find that irregular textures gave weaker impressions of slant than did regular (redundant) textures (Newman, Whinham, and MacRae, 1973).

"Timbre" has also been almost wholly neglected as a target of research. This is in spite of the fact that it is an essential factor in making auditory discriminations. Anyone who has heard Prokofiev's "Peter and the Wolf" knows that the notes of the cat's theme (played by the clarinet) would simply not have the same effect if played by the flute.

One investigator, Lape (1960), has explored "texture" and has shown that estimations of the side-lengths of geometric figures is affected by the texture of the felt edges. In another study, Ekman, et al., (1965) determined that "smoothness" was the inverse of "roughness," and that most individuals prefer smooth objects to rough. Also, it has been shown that a biasing after-effect occurs for both the kinesthetic and visual systems such that after touching (viewing) a piece of course sandpaper, a piece of medium-grade sandpaper feels (appears) coarser than it is (Walker, 1967).

Virtually no research has been done to determine in what ways and to what extent the purity ("essence" here) of olfactory or gustatory stimuli affect perception. Like "timbre," however, the "essence" of an olfactory stimuli can be of crucial importance, especially for individuals engaged in certain pursuits (wine connoisseurs, perfumers, rose breeders, and so on).

Dimension

In the visual system, the *dimensions* of a stimulus is reflected in the sub-modality of "shape." The "shape" of a stimulus is determined by its surface-forming and edge-forming boundaries, and is independent of material, color, texture, and so on. The sub-modality of "form" in the kinesthetic system is directly equivalent to that of visual "shape" (notice, "equivalent"—*not* "equal"). There seems to be no analogical equivalent for *dimension* in the olfactory and gustatory systems, and one would think, not for the auditory system as well. There is, however, an auditory analogue of *dimension* which, if not equivalent to "shape" and "form," at least performs a similar organizing function within the auditory modality. Within the visual system very often it is the "shape" of an object which provides the stimulus with a meaningful context. An array of colors and areas of light and dark usually convey little meaningful information *until* those arrays and areas resolve themselves into characteristics "shapes." In the following examples, the representations are meaningless until you resolve the areas of light and dark into meaningful shape/objects:

(from Thurstone, 1950, p. 7)

Similarly, the kinesthetic system relies upon the "form" of an object in order to make meaning out of the sensations at hand. What "shape" and "form" do for each of these sub-modalities is to *organize* the other expressed sub-modalities by limiting their extent and occurrence. Thus, some "redness" can be organized into six square surfaces with twelve edges and become a *red cube.* The sub-modality which performs a similar function in the auditory system is what I call "patterning." "Patterning" in the auditory modality is the organization of tones, intensities, and timbres into meaningful contexts. In order for auditory stimuli to become meaningful and manipulable its constituents (pitch, intensity, timbre) must be *limited* in terms of *when* each occurs, and for *how long.* It seems reasonable to say, then, that "patterning" provides auditory stimuli with "shape" or "form."

An early study by Revesz (1934) demonstrated that dimensional information in the visual and kinesthetic systems is sufficiently equivalent to allow common visual illusions to be experienced tactually. In his experiment, subjects experienced such visual illusions as the Muller-Lyer illusion by feeling the form of appropriately shaped ridges (see also Day and Avery, 1970). Using visual and tactual equivalents of various patterns, Krauthamer (1968) has explored how well these two modalities share their information. In his study, Krauthamer found that the visual test-object judged against a kinesthetic comparison-object was just as effective as the reverse situation, and that in both cases matching was facilitated by a sequential presentation of the stimuli, rather than a simultaneous presentation. However, *within* each modality, simultaneous presentation of stimuli is more effective for the visual system; and for the kinesthetic system sequential and simultaneous presentation are equally effective.

One significant difference between the visual and kinesthetic modalities is that visual inspection tends to overestimate when estimating size, and tactual handling tends to underestimate (Churchill, 1959). Over (1966) found this same discrepancy between the two modalities when estimating the space between objects as well. In an extension of these experiments, Singer and Day (1969) showed that when a conflict occurs between the felt thickness of an object and its apparent (visual) depth, visual perception will significantly bias haptic depth perception.

This same biasing of kinesthetic judgement by the visual system is apparent in the size-weight illusion. In this illusion, objects of equal weight but of varying apparent size are hefted and estimations made of their relative "heaviness." The consistent finding is that the larger volume objects are perceived to be lighter than the smaller (equally heavy) objects. Bergman (1970) showed that working the opposite direction produces the same results. In his experiment, subjects were blindfolded, given spheres of varying weight, and asked to report as to their relative volumes. The result was that heavier spheres were judged to be of greater volume than the lighter (equal volume) spheres (see also Stevens and Rubin, 1970). The effect is so pervasive that neither suggestions intended to counteract the illusion nor knowledge of the illusion cancel it, but only reduce the range of estimation (Holmberg and Holmberg, 1969).

Several studies have clearly demonstrated that the duration of presentation of a tone is judged to be longer than that for a visual (light) stimulus presented for the same duration. (Also, bright lights were judged to be "on" longer than dim lights.) This perception of longer duration for sounds persisted regardless of stimulus duration, pitch, color, loudness, or band width (Goldstone and Goldfarb, 1964; Goldfarb and Goldstone, 1964). Goldstone and Goldfarb observed that auditory and visual presentations interact such that " . . . equivalent auditory durations act as long anchors on the alternate sense." Later work showed that "empty intervals" bounded by auditory clicks were also judged to be longer than identical intervals bounded by light flashes (unless comparison intervals are provided) (Goldstone and Lhamon, 1972). It was also found that auditory temporal judgements develop before, and facilitate the subsequent learning of, visual temporal discrimination.

When given repetitive two-tone patterns (e.g., HHLLHL $\overline{\text{HHLL}}$ $\overline{\text{HL}}$ . . . . .) to listen to, listeners are able to discriminate the existence of a pattern long before they can describe that pattern (Preusser, 1972; Royer and Garner, 1966). Listeners rapidly organize the repeating tones into the simplest pattern, then continue to hear the tone-series as repetitions of that pattern. Warren (1974) and Warren, et al. (1969) presented subjects with a repeating series of only four different sounds (high-tone/hiss/low-tone/buzz) and found that, although their listeners could discriminate each of the sounds, none could give the correct order better than chance (each sound was 200 msec long). This effect persisted even though each sound was first identified and labeled, and the second tone replaced with a "whistle." A loop of four digits at 200 msec/digit was easily recognized.

Location

A fifth intrinsic class of information conveyed by a stimulus is that of *location*. Whether it originates externally or internally, every stimulus is located in a particular place—even if that location is temporary and that place is "all around." All of the senses have as a sub-modality "location" since the location of the origin of a stimulus is undeniably one of the primary functions of sensory systems.

In the visual system, a stimulus is located by establishing its position relative to other simultaneously observed stimuli. Notice that this simultaneously occurring array of stimuli can be either actually observed or "observed" as an internal picture. Kinesthetic "location" relies upon the body as a point of reference (unlike the visual system which relies upon the external world for its referential points). Thus, events which are perceived through the kinesthetic system are perceived as occurring at, or within, the boundaries of one's body (it is interesting to note here that objects which are attached to one's body seem to extend the body's boundaries—when you hold a stick and tap things with it, you feel those taps and touched surfaces *at the business end of the stick*). In the auditory system phase differences and changes in intensity and pitch provide information as to "location." "Locating" in the olfactory and gustatory systems is probably determined by concentration gradients.

The point at which there is great interaction between the visual and kinesthetic systems occurs in the perception of personal location and orientation in space. The well-known rod-and-frame experiments have made famous the fact that proprioceptive feedback and visual input are mutually dependent upon one another in providing orientation information. For both lateral and backward body tilts, subjects overcompensate for vertical at moderate tilts and undercompensate at more extreme tilts (Ebenholtz, 1970). Groberg, Dustman, and Beck (1969) distinguished between proprioceptive feedback and vestibular feedback, and found that at moderate body tilts most individuals rely on vestibular information, while at more extreme tilts (or if blindfolded) individuals rely on proprioceptive information for judgements of orientation. Grobert, et al., also indicate that when vestibular and proprioceptive cues are inconsistent (i.e., both the head and body tilted, but at different angles) people rely on visual cues to resolve the conflict. Similarly, Dichgan, Diener, and Brandt (1974) found that visual stimulation has no effect upon the perception of verticality, but that as the head tilts the influence of the visual system upon orientation perception increases.

Proprioception and kinesthesis can also greatly affect visual perception. For example, in the "inverted T" (⊥) and the "L" illusions, the vertical line appears to be longer than the equal-length horizontal line when the observer is upright. But when the observer is horizontal, the illusion reverses and the horizontal line appears relatively longer (Day and Avery, 1976). In particular, eye movements seem to be intimately connected with visual processing. Mack and Bachant (1969) found good correlation between spontaneous and controlled eye movements and the subject's report of afterimage movements. (Afterimages are also qualitatively and durationally affected by head and body movements; see Davies,1973). More important are Hall's (1972) findings which showed that eye movements during recall often follow those movements made during stimulus presentation, and that these eye movements aid recall. Inadvertently, Mainwaring (1932) demonstrated that visual and kinesthetic cues are usually involved in recalling auditory experiences. In another early study, Goodfellow (1933) found that using eye movements and a calibrated perimeter was more accurate for locating sound sources than was directional pointing (except between 60° and 75° to the left or right-?). In a series of experiments, Jones (1975) and Jones and Kabanoff (1975) demonstrated that eye movement affects sound localization accuracy. Children and adults are better able to locate a sound source when they are able to see it, as opposed to being blindfolded (reaction time is also faster). If the observer is able to see, but is told to visually fixate a spot or is cued away by an extraneous light source, there is an accompanying decrease in localization accuracy (there is no decrease, however, if the distracting cue is tactile).

In fact, it would seem that the visual, kinesthetic, and auditory systems rely upon extensive inter-correlation of their information in order to provide accurate discriminations of stimulus location. In addition to the studies already cited, a study by Pick, Warren, and Hay (1969) demonstrated that, when judging azimuth, the visual system biases proprioceptive and auditory judgements, and that proprioception can bias auditory and visual judgements (see also Fisher, 1968; Jordon, 1968; and Warren and Pick, Jr., 1970). Also, Mikaelian (1969) found that auditory displacement creates systematic hand coordination displacement (although the effect is not as marked as occurs when displacement occurs in the visual system).

Kinesthetic cues have been found to affect auditory localization. Karrer and Davidson (1967) found that the "A effect" for head rotation and the displacement of an auditory signal (that is, the origin of a sound is displaced from the midline in the same direction as one's head is turned). If a listener's body is tilted 30° to the left or right, the midline (located by sound) is actually displaced to the side opposite that of the tilt—the effect is even greater with a 60° tilt (Comalli and Altshuler, 1971). These same investigators found that body tilt had no effect on midline localization if the sound is presented dichotically through earphones (Comalli and Altshuler, 1971), and that displacement of the auditory midline due to body tilt progressively increases from age five-and-a-half to age seventeen (Altshuler and Comalli, 1970).

Held and Freedman (1963) showed that gross body movements affect sound localization accuracy. In their experiments, subjects who were ambulatory or were allowed head movements while listening to "white noise" for one hour demonstrated a large decrement in their subsequent ability to locate dichotically presented "clicks" (subjects regained normal functioning after about a half hour). If, however, the subject was inactive, or passively moved about during the white noise exposure, there was no decrement in localizing accuracy (see also Freedman and Zacks, 1964). Again, such studies indicate that one's ability to accurately locate the origin of stimuli is dependent upon the modalities constantly recalibrating off of each other's information.

Deutsch has produced several interesting investigations on an illusion of sound localization (1974). In her experiments, subjects listened to dichotically presented tones which oscillated without interval between the left and right ears (a 400hz tone was directed to the left ear and an 800hz tone to the right—tone duration was 250 msec). Under these conditions, most right-handed subjects and some left-handed subjects heard *only* the high tone in the right ear, then shifted to hearing *only* the low tone in the left ear. Right-handed subjects also tended to hear only one tone oscillating from ear to ear. Left-handed subjects, on the other hand, tended to hear "complex" illusions, such as two tones alternating in one ear. An interesting finding is that when Deutsch reversed the pattern (so that the 800hz tone was played to the left ear and the 400hz tone to the right ear), most listeners continued to hear the higher tone as coming into the right ear. The use of earphones or speakers as sound sources had no effect on the illusion. A similar illusion was reported by Pedley and Harper (1959) who demonstrated that, when judging the vertical location of sound sources, subjects locate relatively high tones higher in the visual field and relatively low tones lower in the visual field.

Such intra-modality effects also occur in the visual and kinesthetic systems. For instance, a luminous vertical line which is objectively straight ahead will appear so until that line becomes the edge of a rectangle. It then appears to shift in a direction opposite to the body of the rectangle (Bruell and Albee, 1956). As an example in the kinesthetic system, Wapner, Werner, and Comalli (1958) demonstrated that sensations of touch, cold, and warmth decrease the felt distance between one's nose and cheekbone.

Hypnosis and Synesthesia

Some preliminary experiments on specifying synesthesia patterns have been done by this author. In all of these experiments hypnosis was used in order to effect a light to medium trance in each of the subjects. This approach was taken because it was felt that the concentration of attention and enhanced creativity that normally occurs in the trance state would be conducive to the task at hand.

The purpose of these preliminary investigations was to experiment with the kinds of approaches which might prove useful in determining patterns of synesthesia, and to get an indication of the range of responses which might be expected. Consequently, the research mentioned here is not at all rigorous in conception or execution, but is intended to be indicative of the turns which future work might profitably take.

Very simply, an experimental session consisted of manipulating the subject's experience so that he or she had the opportunity to witness the effect of one sub-modality upon another. Once in trance, subjects were asked to attend to a particular sub-modality (for example: "see a field of blue"). When he/she indicated readiness, an experience from another sub-modality was added by the experimenter (for example, a needle prick, deep pressure, an auditory tone, and so on). The subjects then reported what changes, if any, occurred for them in the sub-modality initially attended to. The twelve subjects (none of whom had any formal knowledge of synesthesia patterns) ranged in age from thirteen to fifty years of age.

Using this experimental format, the easiest procedure was to have the subject visualize fields of colors or shapes, and then to manipulate the kinesthetic and auditory sub-modalities. (All of the responses will not be reported here—only the "trends.") When visualizing "fields" of color or geometric shapes, several individuals reported them to shrink or partially disappear to one side in response to deep pressure on an arm. Deep pressure also caused low frequency colors to lighten (black → dark brown, orange → yellow, red → yellow) and higher frequency colors to darken (creme → "dark," blue → "dark"). In contrast, "light pressure" on the arm was reported by some to cause the field or form to expand or fade. Also, most colors were observed to become "muggy," "grey," and "paler" in response to light pressure. In response to a cool piece of metal on the cheek, several individuals reported colors to pale, while in some a warm piece of metal induced a "deepening" of colors. When pressed on the arm with a pin point, some observed colors to become dull and/or darker, while others had their images disappear.

The note from a tuning fork (A-440) was also used in conjunction with imagery. If the sound source moved, some reported that the image appeared to be "lighter" in the direction corresponding to the sound's origin and/or appear to move in the opposite direction. Like deep pressure, some of the individuals observed that their imaginal field shrank when the sound source was heard to come towards them. A static (unmoving) sound produced many patterns, but a couple of subjects reported that the sound imparted a "wavy texture" to their images. In general, the test note A-440 made blue and black lighter in color, red and yellow darker in color, and did not affect white. In some cases an imagined color was seen to "lighten" as the subject heard tones go from low to high pitchs, while in other cases the colors would change their spectral frequency (usually getting "higher" in frequency).

Few changes were reported when kinesthetic and auditory sub-modalities were paired with one another. A couple of responses were that deep and light pressure caused the A-440 tone to become "softer," while the pin point caused the note to become louder.

Another approach towards defining synesthesia patterns which was tried was to temporarily "eliminate" different sub-modalities in individuals while in deep trance (see Erickson, in Haley, 1967, for details regarding this strategy). Once the perception of a particular sub-modality has been eliminated, the individual can be tested for consequent effects in the other sub-modalities. Following are some of the synesthesia changes reported by those who were successful at eliminating a sub-modality:

Perceptual System Eliminated	Resulting Patterns
color	tunnel vision, lack of depth perception and balance perception
color	lack of depth perception, yellow light appeared to pulsate, colors appeared more intense afterwards
color	no body sensations, hearing acute, no internal dialogue

brightness	lack of depth perception, colors dull, yellow light appeared to be "fire" (became hot and sweated)
added vivid colors	decrease in auditory perception
pitch	unable to distinguish volume changes
pitch	unable to distinguish volume and brightness changes
hearing	increased visual images and brightness changes
proprioception	reduced ability to balance, no perception of taste or pain
light touch in lower half of body	no changes
olfaction	no kinesthetic perception
olfaction	became visually aware of textures
olfaction	olfaction more acute afterwards
olfaction and taste	saw waves when heard another's voice lowering, light appeared brighter when voice raised

Notice that in two of the three color elimination cases that depth perception was impaired as well, and that kinesthesis was also affected in two of the cases. Similarly, in both cases in which pitch discrimination was eliminated, volume perception was also impaired. Impairment of brightness discrimination also affected depth perception was impaired as well, and that kinesthesis was listed above, the impairment of one modality often enhanced another (and, as in the case of the "added vivid color," the enhancement of a modality may impair another).

Though meager, these preliminary findings indicate two things. First, that the sub-modalities do indeed affect and correlate with one another in various ways (which we still have to specify). And second, that hypnosis can be combined with human creativity to provide a means of, perhaps, eventually specifying characteristic patterns of synesthesia. The experimental reports and research to date indicates that there is probably a wide variety of synesthesia patterns, many or most of which may be unique to each individual. But it is also obvious that there are patterns which are generally applicable, and, with a new framework within which to work, we can now begin to ferret those out.

Summary

The purpose of this appendix is to stimulate interest in research on perception at the sub-modality level. For the most part, researchers have not explicitly recognized the effects of *representational systems, sub-modalities,* and *synesthesia patterns* in and upon their research.

Selective attention to sensory input (representational systems) and variations in experience with sensory input (synesthesia patterns) are the two most significant processes responsible for differentiating experiences among individuals. While representational systems determine the domain of sensory information attended to, synesthesia patterns provide the subsequent perceptions with *meaning.* "Meaningfulness" is the result of the inter-correlation of perceptual experiences. Such inter-correlations are patterned (that is, become generalizations of experience), and may be either arbitrarily or inherently determined (language vs. direct experience). Inherent patterns may be the result of associations present in the environment and/or genetically determined. Some of these patterns are the unique products of the experiences of each individual, while other patterns are generally descriptive of human perceptual functioning.

Defining these patterns is important since (1) they are the building blocks with which all experiences are built, and (2) the ways in which they interact affects variables in an analysis of any experiment on perception. As experimenters become cognizant of the intrinsic and crucial role played by sub-modality interactions in creating experiences, perhaps future research will be able to characterize human perception in ways which are truly representative and generative.

REFERENCE LIST

REFERENCE LIST

The following list of references includes both those studies cited in the appendix and additional studies on sensory systems.

General References:

Bach-y-Rita, P. 1972. *Brain Mechanisms in Sensory Substitution.* New York: Academic Press.

Bandler, R., and Grinder, J. 1975. *Patterns of the Hypnotic Techniques of Milton H. Erickson, M.D., Vol. 1.* Cupertino, California: Meta Publications.

Bekesy, G. von. 1957. The ears. *Scientific American.*

Brooks, C.R. 1968. Spatial and verbal components of the art of recall. *Canadian Journal of Psychology.* 22(5): 349-368.

Burley, T. 1973. An investigation of the roles of imagery kinesthetic cues, and attention in tactile nonverbal communication. *Dissertation Abstracts International.* 33 (8b) 3930.

Butters, N., and Brody, B. A. 1969. The role of the left parietal lobe in the mediation of intra- and cross-modal associations. *Cortex.* 4(4):328-343.

Child, I., and Wendt, G. 1938. The temporaral course of the influence of visual stimulation upon the auditory threshold. *Journal of Experimental Psychology.* 23(2):109-127.

Cleaves, W. T., Intramodal and intermodal pattern recognition of multidimensional stimuli. *Dissertation Abstracts International.* 1971. 32(5-B):3024-3025.

Colavita, F. B. 1974. Human sensory dominance. *Perception and Psychophysics.* 16(2):409.

Connolly, K., and Jones, B. 1970. A developmental study of afferent-reafferent integration. *British Journal of Psychology.* 61(2):259-266.

Conrad, R. 1964. Acoustic confusions in immediate memory. *British Journal of Psychology.* 55(1):75-84.

Duncan-Johnson, C., and Coles, M. 1974. Heart rate and disjunctive reaction time: The effects of discrimination requirements. *Journal of Experimental Psychology.* 103(6):1160.

Eccles, J. (ed.). 1966. *Brain and Conscious Experience.* New York: Springer-Verlag.

Gellhorn, E. 1964. Motion and emotion: The role of proprioception in the physiology and pathology of the emotions. *Psychological Review.* 71(6):457-472.

Gibson, J. 1966. *The Senses Considered as Perceptual Systems.* Boston: Houghton-Mifflin Co.

Gilbert, G. M. 1941. Intersensory facilitation and inhibition. *The Journal of General Psychology.* 24:381-407.

Gregory, R. L. 1966. *Eye and Brain.* New York: World Univ. Press.

Grinder, J., and Bandler, R. 1976. *The Structure of Magic, Vol. 2.* Palo Alto, California: Science and Behavior Books.

Haagen-Smith, A. 1952. Smell and taste. *Scientific American.* 186(3):2832.

Hall, D. C. 1972. The effect of eye movement on the recall of information with visual imagery. *Dissertation Abstracts International.* 33(1-B):461-462.

Henion, K. E. 1970. Cross-modal congruity: Visual and olfactory. *Journal of Social Psychology.* 80(1):15-23.

Hess, G. H., and Polt, (article untitled). *Science.* 140:1190. 1964.

Hess, G. H., and Polt, J. M. 1966. Changes in pupil size as a measure of taste difference. *Perceptual and Motor Skills.* 23(2):451-455.

Hillyard, S. A.; Hink, R. F.; Schwent, V. L.; and Picton, T. W. 1973. Electrical signs of selective attention in the human brain. *Science.* 182:177-179.

Jones, B. 1973. When are vision and kinaesthesis comparable? *British Journal of Psychology.* 64(4): 587-591.

Kahneman, D., and Beatty, I. 1966. Pupil diameter and load on memory. *Science.* 154:1583.

Kubovy, M.; Cutting, J.E.; and McGuire, P. M. 1974. Hearing with the third ear. Science. 186:272-274.

Lackner, J. and Garrett, M. 1972. Resolving ambiguity: Effects of biasing context in the unattended ear. *Cognition.* 1(4):359-372.

London, I. D. 1954. Research on sensory interaction in the Soviet Union. *Psychological Bulletin.* 51:531-568.

Mainwaring, J. 1932. Kinaesthetic factors in the recall of musical experiences. *British Journal of Psychology.* 23:284-307.

Marks, L. 1975. On colored hearing synesthesia: Cross-modal translations of sensory dimensions. *Psychological Bulletin.* 82(3).

Marks, L. 1975. Synesthesia: the lucky people with mixed up senses. *Psychology Today.* (June):48-52.

Masterton, R. B., and Berkley, M. A. 1974. Brain function: changing ideas on the role of sensory, motor, and association cortex in behavior. *Annual Review of Psychology.* 25:277-312.

McDonnell, P. M., and Duffett, J. 1972. Vision and touch: a reconsideration of conflict between the two senses. *Canadian Journal of Psychology.* 26(2):171-180.

Metelli, F. 1974. The perception of transparency. *Scientific American.* 230(4):90-98.

Miller, G. A. 1956. The magical number seven, plus or minus two: Some limits on our capacity for processing information. *Psychological Review.* 63:81-97.

Milner, P. 1970. *Physiological Psychology*. New York: Holt, Rinehart & Winston.

Nafe, J. P. 1924. An experimental study of the affective qualities. *American Journal of Psychology*. 35:507-544.

O'Connor, N., and Hermelin, B. 1972. Seeing and hearing and space and time. *Perception and Psychophysics*. 11(1a):46-48.

Perky, C. W. 1910. An experimental study of imagination. *American Journal of Psychology*. 21:422-452.

Pribram, K. 1971. *Languages of the Brain*. Englewood Cliffs, NJ: Prentice-Hall.

Riggs, L., and Karwoski, T. 1934. Synesthesia. *British Journal of Psychology*. 25:29-41.

Rollins, H. A., Schuman, D. L., Evans, M., and Knoph, K. 1975. Human learning and memory. *Journal of Experimental Psychology*. 104(2):173-181.

Ryan, T. A. 1940. Interrelations of sensory systems in perception. *Psychological Bulletin*. 37:659-698.

Santos, J., Farrow, B., and Haines, J. 1965. Consistency and style of autokinetic movement. *Perceptual and Motor Skills*. 21:583-586.

Schiffrin, R. M. and Grantham, D. W. 1974. Can attention be allocated to sensory modalities? *Perception and Psychophysics*. 15(3):460-474.

Scott, Ian. 1969. *The Luscher Color Test*. New York: Random House.

Shipley, T. and Jones, R. W. 1969. Initial observations on sensory interactions and the theory of dyslexia. *Journal of Communication Disorders*. 2(4):295-311.

Thurstone, L. L. 1950. Some primary abilities in visual thinking. *Psychometric Laboratory, University of Chicago*. No. 59 (August 1950).

Warren, D., and Pick, Jr., H. 1970. Intermodality relations in localizations in blind and sighted people. *Perception and Psychophysics*. 8(6):430:432.

Warren, R. M. 1970. Perceptual restoration of missing speech sounds. *Science.* 167:392.

Wicker, F. W. 1968. Mapping the intersensory regions of perceptual space. *Journal of Psychology.* 81(2):178-188.

Young, P. T. 1927. Studies in affective psychology. *American Journal of Psychology.* 38(2):157-193.

Development:

Blank, M., and Klig, S. 1970. Dimensional learning across sensory modalities in nursery school children. *Journal of Experimental Psychology.* 9(2):166-173.

Carterette, E. C., and Jones, M. 1967. Visual and auditory information processing in children and in adults. *Science.* 156:986-988.

Milne, A. M. 1969. A developmental study of touch and vision: form learning and cross-modal transfer. *Dissertation Abstracts.* 29(7b):2656.

Roberts, T. 1975. Skills of analysis and synthesis in early stages of reacting. *British Journal of Educational Psychology.* 45(1):3-9.

Rudel, R. G., and Teuber, H. L. 1964. Cross-modal transfer of shape discrimination by children. *Neuropsychologia.* 2:1-8.

Spencer, C. D. 1970. Life span changes in intersensory and intrasensory integrative functioning. *Dissertation Abstracts International* 30(9b):4402.

Frequency:

Beck, J., and Shaw, W. A. 1962. Magnitude estimation of pitch. *Journal of the Acoustical Society of America.* 34:92-98.

Berry, P. 1961. Effect of colored illumination upon perceived temperature. *Journal of Applied Psychology.* 45(4):248-250.

Bevan, W., and Dukes, W. 1953. Color as a variable in the judgement of size. *American Journal of Psychology.* 66:283-288.

Birren, F. 1950. *Color Psychology and Color Therapy.* New York: McGraw-Hill.

Chamberlain, P. T. 1974. Pitch and relation in recognition of music-like structures. *Perceptual and Motor Skills.* 34(2):419-428.

Holt-Hansen, K. 1968. Taste and pitch. *Perceptual and Motor Skills.* 27:59-68.

Karwoski, T., and Odbert, H. 1938. Color-music. *Psychological Monographs.* 50(2):60-274.

Lie, Ivar. 1969. Psychophysical invariants of achromatic colour vision: 1) the multi-dimensionality of achromatic colour experience. *Scandanavian Journal of Psychology.* 10(3):167-175.

Loewenstein, A., and Donald, G. 1941. A color stereoscopic phenomenon. *Arch. Ophthal.* 26:551-564.

McCain, C. and, Karr, A. 1970. Color and subjective distance. *U. S. Army Human Engineering Lab., Tech. Memorandum No. 20.*

Morgan, G.; Goodson, F.; and, Jones, T. 1974. Age differences in the associations between felt temperatures and color choices. *American Journal of Psychology.* 88(1):125-130.

Nash, C. B. 1969. Cutaneous perception of color. *Journal of the American Society for Psychological Research.* 63(1):83-87.

Payne, M. 1958. Apparent weight as a function of color. *American Journal of Psychology.* 71:724-730.

Payne, M. 1961. Apparent weight as a function of hue. *American Journal of Psychology.* 74:104-105.

Plack, J., and Shick, J. 1974. The effects of color on human behavior. *Association for the Study of Perception.* 9(1):4-16.

Podolsky, E. 1938. *The Doctor Prescribes Colors.* New York: National Library Press.

Sato, T. 1955. The effect of color on the perception of size. *Tohoku Psychologica Folia.* 14:115-129.

Thurlow, W. 1943. Studies in auditory theory. *Journal of Experimental Psychology.* 32:17-36.

Velhagen, K. 1936. Chromatic asthenopia by hypoxemia, a latent disturbance of the color sense. *Arch. Augenheilk.* 109:605-621.

Vicente, J. V., and Vincente, M. L. 1968. Do colors influence taste? *Revista Interamericana de psiocologia.* 23:143-157.

Wallis, C. P., and Audley, R. J. 1964. Response instructions and the speed of relative judgement: II pitch discrimination. *British Journal of Psychology.* 55(2):121-132.

Wallis, W. A. 1935. The influence of color on apparent size. *Journal of General Psychology* 13:193-199.

Intensity:

Ades, H.; Graybiel, A.; Morrill, S.; Tolhurst, G.; and Niven, J. 1958. Non-auditory effects of high-intensity sound stimulation on deaf human subjects. *Journal of Aviation Medicine.* 29:454-467.

Audley, R. J., and Wallis, C. P. 1964. Response instructions and the speed of relative judgements. I. some experiments in brightness discrimination. *British Journal of Psychology.* 55(1):59-73.

Bond, B., and Stevens, S. S. 1969. Cross-modality matching of brightness to loudness by 5-year-olds. *Perception and Psychophysics.* 6(61):337-339.

Ekman, G.; Berglund, B.; and Berglund, U. 1966. Loudness as a function of the duration of auditory stimulation. *Scandanavian Journal of Psychology.* 7(3):201-208.

Halverson, H. 1924. Tonal volume as a function of intensity. *American Journal of Psychology.* 35:360-367.

Kingsbury, B. A. 1927. A direct comparison of the loudness of pure tones. *Physiological Review.* 29:588-600.

Marks, L. 1974. On associations of light and sound: the mediation of brightness, pitch and loudness. *American Journal of Psychology.* 87(1-2):173-188.

McFarland, R. 1971. Enhancement of thermal estimates by concommitant pressure stimulation. *Journal of Experimental Psychology.* 88(1):20-25.

Morgan, C. T.; Garner, W.; and Galambo, R. 1951. Pitch and intensity. *Journal of the Acoustical Society of America.* 23:658-663.

Rich, G. J. 1916. A preliminary study of tonal volume. *Journal of Experimental Psychology.* 1:13-22.

Smith, E. L., and Laird, D. A. 1930. The loudness of auditory stimuli which affect stomach contractions in healthy human beings. *Journal of the Acoustical Society of America.* 2:94-98.

Smith, K., and Hardy, A. 1961. Effects of context on the subjective equation of auditory and visual intensities. *Science.* 134:1623-1624.

Stevens, J., and Marks, L. 1965. Cross-modality matching of brightness and loudness. *Proceedings of the National Academy of Sciences.* 54(2):407-411.

Stevens, S. S. 1934. Tonal density. *Journal of Experimental Psychology.* 17:585-592.

Stevens, S. S. 1934. The volume and intensity of tones. *American Jouranl of Psychology.* 46:397-408.

Stevens, S. S. 1936. The relation of pitch to intensity. *Journal of Accoustical Society of America.* 6:150-159.

Stevens, S. S., and Poulton, E. C. 1956. The estimation of loudness by unpracticed observers. *Journal of Experimental Psychology.* 51(1):71-78.

Terrace, H. S., and Stevens, S. S. 1962. The quantification of tonal volume. *American Journal of Psychology.* 75(4):596-604.

Zahn, J. R., and Haines, R. F. 1971. The influence of central search task luminance upon peripheral visual detection time. *Psychological Science.* 24(6):271-273.

Purity:

Ekman, G.; Hosman, J.; and Lindstrom, B. 1965. Roughness, smoothness, and preference: a study of quantitative relations in individual subjects. *Journal of Experimental Psychology.* 70(1):18-26.

Hunton, V., and Sumner, F. 1948. The affective tone of tactual impressions. *The Journal of Psychology.* 26:235-242.

Newman, C. V.; Whinhan, E. A., and MacRae, A. W. 1973. The influence of texture on judgements of slant and relative distance in a picture with suggested depth. *Perception and Psychophysics.* 14(2):280-284.

Panek, D., and Stevens, S. S. 1966. Saturation of red: a prothetic continuum. *Perception and Psychophysics.* 1(2):59-66.

Pitt, I. T., and Winter, L. M. 1974. Effect of surround on perceived saturation. *Journal of the Optical Society of America* 64(10):1328-1331.

Walker, J. T. 1967. Textural after-effects: tactual and visual. *Dissertation Abstracts.* 28(6b):2649.

Form:

Abravanel, E. 1971. The synthesis of length within and between perceptual systems. *Perception and Psychophysics.* 9(4):327-328.

Appelle, S. 1971. Visual and haptic angle perception in the matching task. *American Journal of Psychology.* 84(4):487-499.

Bergman, L. 1970. On Usnadze's volume illusion. *Psychologische Forschung.* 33(4):310-324.

Butter, E. J., and Zung, B. J. 1970. A developmental investigation of the effect of sensory modality on form recognition in children. *Developmental Psychology.* 3(2):276.

Churchill, A. V. 1959. A comparison of tactual and visual interpolation. *Canadian Journal of Psychology.* 13(1):23-27.

Clegg, J. M. 1971. Verbal transformations on the repeated listening to some English consonants. *British Journal of Psychology.* 62(3):303-309.

Coltheart, M. 1969. The influence of haptic size information upon visual judgements of absolute distance. *Perception and Psychophysics.* 5(3):143-144.

Davidson, P.; Abbott, S.; and Gershenfeld, J. 1974. Influence of exploration time on haptic and visual matching of complex shapes. *Perception and Psychophysics.* 15(3):539-543.

Day, R., and Avery, G. 1970. Absence of the horizontal and vertical illusion in haptic space. *Journal of Experimental Psychology.* 83(1):172-173.

Deutsch, D. 1974. An auditory illusion. *Nature.* 251:307-309.

Dowling, W. 1971. Recognition of inversions of melodies and melodic contours. *Perception and Psychophysics.* 9(3b):348-349.

Dowling, W. 1972. Recognition of melodic transformations. *Perception and Psychophysics.* 12(5):417-421.

Holmberg, L., and Holmberg, I. 1969. The psychophysics of the size-weight illusion: IV and the relation to secondary suggestibility. *Psychological Research Bulletin.* 9(4):7.

Karwoski, T., Odbert, H., and Osgood, C. 1942. Studies in synesthesic thinking II. The role of form in visual responses to music. *Journal of General Psychology.* 26:199-122.

Koseleff, P. 1958. Studies in the perception of heaviness. *Acta Psychologica.* 14(2):109-130.

Krauthamer, G. 1959. Form perception across sensory modalities. *American Psychologist.* 14:396.

Krauthamer, G. 1968. Form perception across sensory modalities. *Neuropsychologia.* 6:105-113.

Lape, I. 1960. Measuring function of the hand. *Dokl. Akad. Pedag. Nauk RSFSR.* 5:53-56.

Lass, N.; West, L.; and Taft, D. 1973. A non-verbal analogue to the verbal transformation effect. *Canadian Journal of Psychology.* 27(3):272-279.

Miller, E. 1972. Interaction of vision and touch in conflict and non-conflict form perception tasks. *Journal of Experimental Psychology.* 96(1):114-123.

Moul, E. 1930. An experimental study of visual and auditory thickness. *American Journal of Psychology.* 42:544-560.

Obusek, C. J. 1972. An experimental investigation of some hypotheses concerning the verbal transformation effect. *Dissertation Abstracts International.* 32(7b): 4257.

Over, R. 1966. Relationships between visual, haptic, and tactile judgements of some illusion figures. *Australian Psychologist.* 1(1):92.

Peterson, L.; Holsten, J.; and Spevak, P. 1975. Spatial coding of auditory signals. *Memory and Cognition.* 3(3):243-246.

Pollack, R. 1964. The effects of fixation upon the apparent magnitude of bounded horizontal extent. *American Journal of Psychology.* 77(2):177-192.

Preusser, D. 1972. The effect of structure and rate on the recognition and description of auditory temporal pattern. *Perception and Psychophysics.* 11(3):233-240.

Revesz, G. 1934. System der optischen und haptischen raumtauschung. *Z. Psychol.* 131:296-375.

Royer, F., and Garner, W. 1966. Response uncertainty and perceptual difficulty of auditory temporal patterns. *Perception and Psychophysics.* 1(2):41-47.

Singer, G., and Day, R. 1969. Visual capture of haptically judged depth. *Perception and Psychophysics.* 5(5): 315-316.

Stevens, J. C., and Rubin, L. 1970. Psychophysical scales of apparent heaviness and the size-weight illusion. *Perception and Psychophysics.* 8(4):225-230.

Wapner, S., Werner, H., and Commalli, Jr. P. 1958. Effect of enhancement of head boundary on head size and shape. *Perceptual and Motor Skills.* 8:319-325.

Warren, R. 1974. Auditory pattern recognition by untrained listeners. *Perception and Psychophysics.* 15(3):495.

Warren, R.; Obusek, C.; and Farmer, R. 1969. Auditory sequence: confusion of pattern other than speech and music. *Science.*

Localization:

Altshuler, M., and Comalli, P. 1970. Auditory localization and body tilt. *Journal of Auditory Research.* 10:197-200.

Bekesy, G. von. 1938. The origin of the perception of distance in hearing. *Akust. Z.* 3:21-31.

Bekesy, G. von. 1949. The moon illusion and similar auditory phenomena. *American Journal of Psychology.* 62:540-552.

Bourdon, B. 1925. Some experiments on auditory space perception. *Annee Psychol.* 26:72-78.

Bruell, J. H., and Albee, G. W. 1956. A new illusion of apparent movement and the concept of retinal local signs. *Journal of Psychology.* 41:55-59.

Butter, R. 1973. The relative influence of pitch and timbre on the apparent location of sound in the median sagittal plane. *Perception and Psychophysics.* 14(2): 255-258.

Coleman, P. 1963. An analysis of hues with auditory depth perception in free space. *Psychological Bulletin.* 60(3):302-315.

Comalli, P. Jr., and Altshuler, M. 1971a. Effect of body tilt on auditory localizations. *Perceptual and Motor Skills.* 32(3):723-726.

Comalli, P. Jr., and Altshuler, M. 1971b. Effect of body tilt on auditory lateralization. *Perceptual and Motor Skills.* 32(3):767-772.

Davies, P. 1973. Effects of movements on the appearance and duration of a prolonged visual after-image. *Perception* 2(2):155-160.

Dichgan, J.; Diener, H.; and Brandt, Th. 1974. Optokinetic-Graviceptibe interaction in different head positions. *Acta Oto-Laryngologica.* 78(5)-6:391-398.

Ebenholtz, S. 1970. Perception of the verticle with body tilt in the median plane. *Journal of Experimental Psychology.* 83(1)-1:1-6.

Fisher, G. 1966. Autokinesis in vision, auditon, and tactile-kinaesthesis. *Perceptual and Motor Skills.* 22:470.

Fisher, G. 1968. Agreement between the spatial senses. *Perceptual and Motor Skills.* 26:849-850.

Freedman, S., and Zacks, J. 1964. Effects of active and passive movement upon auditory function during prolonged atypical stimulation. *Perception and Motor Skills.* 18-361-366.

Geissler, L. 1915. Sound localization under determined expectation. *American Journal of Psychology.* 76:268-285.

Gescheider, G. 1965. Cutaneous sound localization. *Journal of Experimental Psychology.* 70(6):617-625.

Gescheider, G. 1970. Some comparisons between touch and hearing. *IEEE Transactions on Man-Machine Systems.* MMS-11(1):28-35.

Goodfellow, L. 1933. An empirical comparison of the various techniques used in the study of the localization of sound. *Journal of Experimental Psychology.* 16:598-610.

Groberg, D.; Dustman, R.; and Beck, E. 1969. The effect of body and head tilt in the perception of vertical. *Neuropsychologia.* 7:89-100.

Harris, C., and Sommer, H. 1968. Human equilibrium during acoustic stimulation by discreet frequencies. *USAF AMRL Technical Report* #68-7:1-11.

Harris, C. 1965. Perceptual adaptation to inverted, reversed, and displaced vision. *Psychological Review.* 72(6): 419-444.

Held, R., and Freedman, S. 1963. Plasticity in human sensory motor control. *Science.* 142:3591.

Jones, B. 1975. Visual facilitation of auditory localization in school children. *Perception and Psychophysics.* 17(3):217.

Jones, B., and Kabanoff, B. 1975. Eye movements in auditory space perception. *Perception and Psychophysics.* 17(3)241.

Karrer, G., and Davidson, R. 1967. Auditory direction and head rotation. *Perceptual and Motor Skills.* 24(3-1): 961-962.

Mack, A., and Bachant, J. 1969. Perceived movement of the after-image during eye movement. *Perception and Psychophysics.* 6(6-A):379-384.

Mikaelian, H. 1969. Adaptation to rearranged ear-hand coordination. *Perceptual and Motor Skills.* 28(1):147-150.

Mikkonen, V., and Kolehmainen, K. 1968. On the nonvision cues controlling throwing movements. *Scandanavian Journal of Psychology.* 9(3):169-176.

Millar, S. 1972. The development of visual and kinesthetic judgements of distance. *British Journal of Psychology.* 63(2):271-282.

Pedley, P., and Harper, R. 1959. Pitch and the vertical localization of sound. *American Journal of Psychology.* 72:447-449.

Pick, H. Jr.; Warren, D.; and Hay, J. 1969. Sensory conflict in judgements of spatial direction. *Perception and Psychophysics.* 6(4):203-205.

Silver, R. 1969. Tilt after-effects in touch. *Dissertation Abstracts International.* 30(4-b):1931.

Sommer, H., and Harris, C. 1970. Comparative effects of auditory and extra-auditory acoustic stimulation on human equilibrium and motor performance. *USAF AMRL Technical Report.* 70-26:16.

Time:

Bell, C., and Provius, K. 1963. Relations between physiological responses to environmental heat and time judgements. *Journal of Experimental Psychology.* 66(6):572-579.

Danziger, K. 1965. Effect of variable stimulus intensity on estimates of duration. *Perceptual and Motor Skills.* 20:505-508.

Ehrensing, R, and Lhamon, W. 1966. Comparison of tactile and auditory time judgements. *Perceptual and Motor Skills.* 23(3-1):929-930.

Goldfarb, J., and Goldstone, S. 1964. Properties of sound and the auditory-visual difference in time judgement. *Perceptual and Motor Skills.* 19:606.

Goldstone, S., and Goldfarb, J. 1964. Auditory and visual time judgement. *Journal of General Psychology.* 70:369-387.

Goldstone, S., and Lhamon, W. 1972. Auditory-visual differences in human temporal judgement. *Perceptual and Motor Skills.* 34(2):623-633.

Gridley, P. 1932. The discrimination of short intervals of time by fingertip and by ear. *American Journal of Psychology.* 44:18-43.